Praise for *Wired for Joy*

"So many authors today promise to bring joy to your life, help you lose weight, or inspire you to overcome addictions using a magical method that turns out to be completely inapplicable. But **Wired for Joy** *is the real deal! With inspiring anecdotes about real people, clear language, and lovely diagrams,* **Wired for Joy** *delivers a technology—based on more than 30 years of research—that can lift us from the stressed-out state to the natural state of pure joy, where the need for the fixes of food, drink, drugs, and workaholism melt away. I am heartily recommending this book to everyone— this is the one book to read if you have no time to read!"*

— **Candace B. Pert, Ph.D.,** best-selling author of *Molecules of Emotion* and *Everything You Need to Know to Feel Go(o)d*

"A remarkable book by an internationally acknowledged expert in the field of stress management. Laurel Mellin's method for rewiring the emotional brain is revolutionary . . . a practical approach for decreasing stress, enhancing health and happiness, and rediscovering joy! Highly recommended."

— **John Foreyt, Ph.D.,** author of *The Xenical Advantage* and *The Living Heart Diet*; director of the Behavioral Medicine Research Center, Baylor College of Medicine

*"****Wired for Joy*** *offers a brain-based solution to stress and practical tools that are the missing link in health care."*

— **John Gray, Ph.D.,** #1 *New York Times* best-selling author of *Men Are from Mars, Women Are from Venus*

"Chronic stress and anxiety are enormous problems for many people in our fast-paced and rapidly changing society. EBT offers a novel and compelling approach to gaining control over one's life and thereby containing the physiological and psychological toll of chronic stress."

— **Bruce S. McEwen, Ph.D.**, author of *The End of Stress as We Know It;* Alfred E. Mirsky professor; and head of the Harold and Margaret Milliken Hatch Laboratory of Neuroendocrinology, The Rockefeller University

"Laurel Mellin applies the principles of brain-plasticity science to help you grow and nourish your positive energies. Consider it a gift, from science to you."

— **Michael Merzenich, Ph.D.**, neuroscientist and professor emeritus of physiology, University of California, San Francisco

wired
for

joy

Also by Laurel Mellin

The Pathway

The Solution

The 3-Day Solution Plan

The Shapedown Program

wired
for

A Revolutionary Method for Creating Happiness from Within

Laurel Mellin

HAY HOUSE, INC.
Carlsbad, California • New York City
London • Sydney • Johannesburg
Vancouver • Hong Kong • New Delhi

Published and distributed in the United States by: Hay House, Inc.: www.hayhouse.com • *Published and distributed in Australia by:* Hay House Australia Pty. Ltd.: www.hayhouse.com.au • *Published and distributed in the United Kingdom by:* Hay House UK, Ltd.: www.hayhouse.co.uk • *Published and distributed in the Republic of South Africa by:* Hay House SA (Pty), Ltd.: www.hayhouse.co.za • *Distributed in Canada by:* Raincoast: www.raincoast.com • *Published in India by:* Hay House Publishers India: www.hayhouse.co.in

Emotional Brain Training and the EBT 5-Point System are trademarks used under license by the Institute for Health Solutions, a nonprofit organization. A nonprovisional patent is pending for The EBT 5-Point System of Emotional and Behavioral Regulation.

To learn the details of the science behind the method presented in this book, please refer to: **www.ebt.org**.

Design: Jami Goddess   •   *Interior photos:* Joe Mellin and Jamison Design

Library of Congress Cataloging-in-Publication Data

Mellin, Laurel.
  Wired for joy / Laurel Mellin. -- 1st ed.
      p. cm.
  Includes bibliographical references.
  ISBN 978-1-4019-2586-4 (tradepaper : alk. paper) 1. Joy. I. Title.
  BF575.H27M45 2010
  158.1--dc22

                              2010003535

ISBN: 978-1-4019-2586-4

13 12 11 10   4 3 2 1
1st edition, June 2010

FSC
Mixed Sources
Product group from well-managed forests, controlled sources and recycled wood or fiber
Cert no. BV-COC-930557
www.fsc.org
© 1996 Forest Stewardship Council

Printed in the United States of America

For Mackey and Papa

Contents

Chapter 1

A Revolution from Within

Imagine yourself in the spring of the year 2020—the daffodils are in bloom, the weather is gorgeous, there are children playing, and you pick up the paper to find one of the strangest headlines you've ever read: "Drug Companies Having Bake Sales to Raise Funds."

Perhaps you're saying to yourself, *How can this be? What on earth could make drug companies sell coconut cupcakes and chocolate cream pies?* But then you start thinking. Maybe it's those five simple tools—the ones that help you control your emotional brain and keep it from sending you into stress. After all, they have reduced your meltdowns, your jaw clenching, and your late-night refrigerator raids. You are taking fewer and fewer medications as you perfect the use of the tools. But could it be that everyone had started using them?

Wired for Joy introduces you to the five simple tools of emotional brain training (EBT) that help you gain control of your emotional brain, the clearinghouse for regulating the stresses of life. The point of the method is to acquire tools that harness the emotional brain's natural capacity to process daily life. Using these tools creates a revolution from within, decreasing stress symptoms and helping you uncover what lies beneath that stress: joy.

JOY BY CHOICE, NOT CHANCE

The human brain has an amazing capacity to create joy not by chance, but by choice. Everyone has the equipment to do this—and it is uniquely human. Unlike other animals, the human brain has multiple strong connections between areas of conscious thought and pleasure. The thinking brain—the seat of consciousness—is strongly linked to the emotional brain, where pleasure centers abound. You can learn to use your consciousness to send chemicals and electricity through those connections and create ripples of pleasure that you can feel in your body.

There are only two glitches. First, the message that arouses such pleasure cannot be about eating ice cream, sipping fine wine, or buying the latest shoes. It can't be anything you acquire, ingest, or inject. Instead, that pleasure comes from the desire to be of service, to do good. Our hunter-gatherer ancestors survived based on their capacity to cooperate and share. As a result, this *joy response* evolved over the millennia to ensure the survival of the species. When you take action that favors the greater good, you are rewarded in the moment. A pulse of feel-good chemicals affixes to special receptors in the brain's reward centers, and you experience a surge of peace, power, and pleasure in your body.

Second, the system of creating bliss on demand breaks down during stress. Stress hormones affect your motivations, because you are in survival mode. Forget about compassion. Instead, you focus on surviving the moment, doing whatever it takes. In that stressed state, your thinking brain is not functioning well. It is not thinking magnificent thoughts and fueling you with passion to be your most altruistic self. Your emotions, thoughts, and behaviors are decidedly extreme, because even though you are not being chased by a hungry lion, your brain perceives that you are. Survival is the drive, and the chemical cascade is ensuring that you will do whatever you need to do to get what you want when you want it, without regard to how that affects others. That is the nature of the *stress response*. It is ego-based, extreme, and meant for episodic use to keep you alive in response to short-term stressors.

In effect, your physiology is organized around the dance of these two responses: stress and joy. You need both, as short-term survival is based on marshalling an effective *stress* response—in other words, creating a response to make you run away from the approaching lion. And long-term survival is predicated on your capacity to marshal an effective *joy* response. As the feel-good chemicals flow, you feel an abiding compassion for others that motivates cooperation and sharing, essential for enabling your tribe to thrive and not blow up the planet. The problem is that the stress response is not only triggered by physical stress like the lion chasing us but also by metabolic and psychological stress. As a result, you see lions everywhere. The stress response ends up being recruited chronically, and can even cannibalize the joy response, as the brain cannot be in a state of joy and stress at the same time. One of the two swamps the other. This is why the relentless pursuit of natural joy may be the most effective defense against stress.

Stress is both a worldwide epidemic and a highly personal one. Most people are overloaded these days—depressed, anxious, and on edge, with the stress buzzer jammed on. The resulting chronic leakage of stress hormones—that drip, drip, drip—causes extremes of emotions, thoughts, and behaviors. It can impact every organ system in potentially deleterious ways and is the root cause of 80 percent of the health problems and most human suffering. When you gain weight, you blame yourself for eating the extra ice cream or sitting on the couch, but it's stress that fuels those tendencies. When you fall into depression, you imagine that it is some fault of your own; however, research points to the fundamental cause of depression as stress. When stress levels are over the top, you are apt to sprout many stress symptoms, each of which stresses you out and exacerbates the other symptoms more.

The current paradigm of health care looks at each of these problems as a distinct issue rather than a symptom of stress. Doctors treat each one with a different cluster of drugs, devices, or procedures. Though costly, this used to be your best option, but in the last decade the true nature of stress has been decoded, and the mysteries of the brain have become a lot less mysterious. The way has been cleared for a new paradigm to take hold: instead of treating the symptoms of stress we can treat the stress itself. We can address the root cause of many symptoms in one fell swoop.

FINDING THE SOURCE

Over the last 20 years, research has shown that the source of most of our stress is the brain itself. Given the onslaught of stress in daily life, it can easily become wired to favor stress—to amplify the real stress in our lives and manufacture a sense of imminent danger, even when there is none. Each time the stress of the day overwhelms your capacity to effectively process it, there is a price to pay. That price is an increase in your *allostatic load*, the wear and tear in the body and brain due to episodes of stress. That load of stress is cumulative, and given enough episodes of stress, it can turn a perfectly normal brain into one that is stuck in stress, constantly producing cascades of stress hormones. As allostatic load increases, the brain becomes highly sensitized to stress, and in time begins to erode the very structures and processes that were designed to protect you from stress. Then you become a magnate for symptoms. Whether it's blood pressure, back problems, weight gain, infections, stomachaches, sexual problems, depression, anxiety, hostility, relationship problems, addictions, or various compulsions, each stress symptom further increases your stress load. Before you know it, you have organized your life around trying to fix what is wrong with you, and you are so mired in stress that you forget how great you could feel.

The goal of EBT is to reverse your allostatic load by using simple tools that give you the capacity to be at any level of stress and find the precise pathway through the brain back to a state of joy. The more moments you spend in well-being, the more you turn around stress-related increase in allostatic load, and the myriad of stress symptoms tend to improve. The strategy is to rewire self-regulation, the fundamental way we process daily life.

Instead of tolerating feeling stressed out, you identify your level of stress, then choose the corresponding tool to switch your brain back to a state of well-being. You do that again and again over time—for the brain only changes by repeated experience—and at some point you will download into your brain the pathways to move through stress rather than getting stuck it in. You will sense that, at long last, you have an emotional anchor, a safe haven within. You will be free to feel your strong, robust emotions, and at liberty to experience any level of stress, confident that you know just the mental practice that will switch you back to a state of well-being. Things that used to cause you to clench your teeth, raid the refrigerator, scream at your kids, or hole up in the den won't bother you anymore. And most of those issues that you swept under the rug will have disappeared.

At that point, you have become a wizard of you own stress processing, and even though life will still be difficult and you will still find yourself stressed out some of the time; more often than not, you will feel joy regardless of circumstance. It's a wonderful way to live, and it all starts with turning your attention away from problems and toward the elegant act of using precise mental tools to rewire your emotional brain.

SWITCHING THOSE WIRES

When I get into my car in the morning, I put the key into the ignition and turn on the engine. At least that's what I assume I do, since I end up driving to work. But I don't do any of it consciously—it is so automatic that I don't have to think about it. The information that lets me do this is stored in my emotional brain, the unconscious memory storehouse. In fact, most things are stored in our unconscious memory. When humans are faced with a stimulus, we draw upon these unconscious memories of past experiences to respond effectively. These responses are stored as wires. The normal stresses of the day—the coffee spilling, a deadline looming, or a craving for sweets—arouse wires, each of which channels chemicals and electricity along a specific pathway so that we respond the same way that we have in the past.

Those wires fall into two categories. Some of those wires are highly effective—just what you need. We call these *joy circuits*. The coffee spills, and you say, "ouch" and go about cleaning it up and feeling pretty good. You keep your cool and don't let one spilled cup of coffee ruin your day. The other wires—the ones that are not effective—we call *stress circuits*. When they are triggered, that one spilled cup of coffee leads to a burning sense of resentment, having a chip on your shoulder during a meeting, soothing yourself with chocolates, and feeling bloated and grumpy. That's an ineffective wire, arousing unnecessary stress that is prolonged.

What's causing most of your stress is that you have too many stress circuits and too few joy circuits. The strategy in EBT is to use powerful, practical tools to alter that wiring, breaking stress circuits and building joy circuits that move you through stress and make you feel great. EBT is a practice, and although this book introduces you to the practice, these circuits break only over time, with repeated use of the tools. You are rewiring the emotional brain, the center not only of stress processing but also of emotions, intimacy, spirituality, and pleasure drives.

As the tools have their effect and more of the stress circuits fall away, joy circuits will take hold and allow you to gracefully and effectively process daily life. When that occurs, life changes in ways that are nothing less than revolutionary. Using the brain's natural processes, you can rewire your emotional circuitry and make it easy to be in love with your life and to do what you came to earth to do. What could be better than that?

Joy as a Brain State

Often when people first learn about the method, they wonder about this "joy" word. In EBT, we use that word to indicate a brain state, but in actuality, the emotion of joy is just the tip of the iceberg— one sign that your physiology is balanced and your internal workings are at their best. You are present, balanced, and have positive emotions fueled by a sense of meaning in your life. When in joy, the stress response is quiet, the relaxation response is activated, and surges of feel-good chemicals course through the reward pathways in the brain. And this brain state is universal. Whether you are a new mother in Manhattan, a musician in Ghana, a brain surgeon in Des Moines, or a banker in Brazil, the physiology of that state is the same.

It turns out that the emotion that feels the best—joy—is also best for our health and the survival of the species. According to neuroscientist Antonio Damasio, joy is the signpost that we are in a state of optimal coordination and smooth running of the operations of life. Wear and tear is at a minimum, aging slows, and, in every possible way, people are at their best.

It's important, however, to differentiate joy and happiness. It may sound like splitting hairs, but from a brain standpoint, they are extremely different. All moments of joy include an element of happiness. But not all moments of happiness include joy. Happiness often comes from drive reduction—avoidance of pain or the pursuit of pleasure for pleasure's sake. The essence of joy, on the other hand, is spirit. Thomas Merton, a Trappist monk, wrote, "Do not look for rest in any pleasure, because you were not created for pleasure: you were created for joy. And if you do not know the difference between pleasure and joy you have not yet begun to live." Joy is spiritual and far grittier than happiness, and far more robust.

Compare the pleasure of eating pizza to the joy of belly laughing with friends or surrendering to the sweetness of love. Joy is more complex. You are in rapture when seeing the face of your child, but sad that he or she is growing up and will ultimately leave you. You are in awe watching a blazing sunset, but know that soon night will fall and the color will vanish. In that moment of spiritual bliss, you can almost taste the other moments, those of feeling empty and lost. You write the most astonishing poem, definitely inspired, and then put down the pen and fear that you will never write another poem again. Unlike happiness, the underbelly of joy is pain, mirroring the wholeness of life, the interweaving of opposites, the unity of it all. In a way, that pain makes the moment even more riveting, and it intensifies and deepens your joy.

LADDERS IN THE BRAIN

Recently, I was sorting through some boxes in the basement of my house. My children were newly launched, all in college or beyond, so there was finally time for me to look through these bits of memorabilia: the favorite stuffed animals; the drawings of flowers; the bevy of prized books. While I was reminiscing, I happened upon an old tape, a series of recordings I made of the children chatting back and forth, mostly after dinner before baths and bed. To my utter amazement, I listened to my daughter, then about four years old, explain to me that there are ladders in the brain. I started laughing because it turns out that she was right!

Neuroscience has shown that there *are* ladders in the brain, the rungs of which we refer to as *brain states.* Knowing about these brain states gives you insights into how to find the best way to climb out of any stressed state back to the top; that is, back to joy. In each of these brain states, a different part of the brain is in charge, depending on the level of stress. When stress is low, the top part, the neocortex, takes the lead. When overwhelmed with stress, the bottom part, the reptilian brain, is dominant. At intermediate states of stress, areas in between take the lead.

We also know that a person's brain state changes moment to moment throughout the day. When I'm sifting through the memorabilia in the basement, I'm relaxed and joyous, savoring happy memories. The top of my brain is in charge, and I'm feeling in love with my life. If a fat rat came into view as I pored through the old photos, I'd probably jump up, scream, and carry on as if my life were on the line. It doesn't matter if the stress is real or imagined, emotional, physical, or even metabolic. It's all stress. So the brain downshifts, giving control to the more primitive reptilian brain, which is reflective and quick.

If you freeze-framed me languishing in the basement in rapture with happy memories and again when I was screaming and carrying on in response to that rat, you'd think you had caught two different people: one was scared and crazy and the other as sane as they come. I am the same person, but my brain state changed. If we are that different in each of the brain states, imagine how different those brain states are, chemically and electrically.

The vast chemical and electrical differences between the brain states explains why, up to this point, stress management has been so challenging. Most methods are one-size-fits-all. They encourage you to use the same process—self-analysis, positive thinking, and meditating—no matter what your brain state. That worked fine until we began learning more about the brain. Because the brain is so different at each level of stress, it doesn't make sense that the same process would be optimally effective for the times when you are only a little rattled and those when you are completely overwhelmed. If you are really serious about climbing out of stress back to joy, then having customized tools—one for each brain state—only makes sense.

Our research has led us to designate five distinct brain states and five specific tools that consistently and reliably process the stresses of daily life to get you back to a state of well-being. Each brain state is characterized by certain universal thought patterns and ways of processing information. Thus each tool works only for the brain state you are in at that time, which makes the method bidirectional. You can identify your brain state, and then reach for the corresponding tool, or you can try out a tool, and the one that works shows you what brain state you were in.

THE HIGHLY PLASTIC BRAIN

By knowing what brain state you're in and using the tool that opens up your joy, you feel great. But then the feeling passes, and you're back to feeling a little stressed. That's because the emotional brain thrives on the status quo. It likes what it knows and learns to stay at a certain level of stress out of habit. The more moments of the day it spends in stress, the more it likes hanging out there. This becomes its *set point*—the point it fights to get back to. However, we know that this set point can change. After all, the brain is highly plastic. It changes in response to experience, bringing to humans an expansive capacity to adapt to diverse environmental realities.

Yet you will see in the pages that follow that the emotional states of the brain are rather impervious to a strict diet of knowledge, insight, planning, and deciding. You can read a stack of books on parenting but still parent just the way your parents did. You can know every last detail about your childhood but still respond to conflict the same way you used to. You can list all your issues, but listing them doesn't change them. To change your emotional brain requires accessing a fine set of emotional skills, which are presented as the five tools of EBT. No matter what state you're in, these tools bring you back to feeling great.

It is important to have those tools because they make it safer to focus on your feelings. The only way to train the brain to shift its emotional set point is through emotion. You can't think your way to healing a deep hurt. The circuits are emotional, and they only open up and change when you feel your emotions. Often people go to great lengths to avoid feeling their emotions because it scares them. If they felt their sadness it could go into depression, or if they were aware of their anger, it could trigger a sugar binge. The truth is that if you don't have the skills to process emotions, then they *are* dangerous, which is why EBT is based on using effective emotional processing tools.

The emotional brain changes only through experience. And while it is very powerful, it is not all that smart. Because the brain is a creature of habit, it would rather be consistently miserable than periodically happy. From the emotional brain's standpoint, any change is objectionable because the emotional brain confuses safety with the familiar. Anything novel, such as a bright sunny mood, is suspect and, in fact, blips of joy can trigger a full-blown stress response. So the brain resists change, and when asked to change, it hides out, performs poorly, and generally doesn't cooperate. That's where the neocortex shines because it has the capacity to focus attention and use mental practices to switch the brain to joy over and over again. Much like learning to ride a bicycle, using the tools feels a little wobbly at first. But with practice it becomes easier, as the emotional brain follows your lead and learns to favor a state of joy.

And a point arrives when a switch finally flips and joy becomes the brain's set point. The brain begins to feel safe in joy and will work to get back to it—just as it once fought to return to stress. At this point, life becomes organized around experiencing joy in the moment rather than revolving around identifying and fixing problems. Most stress symptoms begin to fade, and you can manage those that remain.

Although changing the emotional brain takes time, simply using the tools will provide moments of pleasure, relief from stress, and fascinating insights. In short, there is joy in the journey!

STANDING THE TEST OF TIME

There is no question in my mind that using these tools, over time, in a focused, intensive way rewires the emotional brain. After conducting research on the method, training thousands of participants, and using it in my own life, the power of brain rewiring is very real to me. When a participant in an EBT group has used the method over time, his or her stress processing changes, even how the person uses the tools changes because the brain now switches back to joy more easily.

The tools you're about to learn have been used and tested, most over a period of more than 30 years. Even though the version you'll be learning is an easier, more effective version of the method, the fundamental aspects of the method have stood the test of time. However, more research is ongoing, and no doubt we will learn more about the method and more about the emotional brain in the years to come.

Wired for Joy brings together ideas from vast bodies research on neuroplasticity, attachment, and stress science, and presents tools that you can use in your own life. Most of the chapters are organized around two themes: The first is the science itself—how the brain works, how to use the tools, how to create new wires. The second is a story to show the application of the tools in action. Although the characters and events I use in these anecdotes are fictional, taking place in the future, their actions and their responses to EBT are composites of the thousands of participants I have worked with.

The End of an Era

Throughout the book, we'll talk more about using the tools and the brain science behind them. But before we do, let's settle back and imagine a future in the year 2020.

The pharmaceutical binge peaked in 2010, when Americans filled approximately 4,545,000,000 prescriptions—16 for every man, woman, and child in the country. The vast majority of these treated the symptoms of stress. As stress symptoms mounted, the drug companies found a pill for every ailment, and prescription drug sales continued to spiral upward, while medication side effects became the fourth leading cause of death in the country. Then, without much fanfare, and a marked absence of national exposés, drug sales began tapering off, until the year 2020. That's the year that the bottom dropped out of the market.

It was hard to put your finger on what made this decline in drug use begin. But there was no denying that there had been a social trend toward people putting down their pill bottles, flushing the extra sleeping pills, and cleaning up their lifestyles—all sensible acts. Increasing one's consciousness about taking care of the brain, sharpening mental skills, and loading up on vitamins for brain health had become popular. Drug companies took notice, but it was not until emotional brain training began catching on that the most forward-thinking drug company czars saw its potential to wreak havoc with demand for their products. Others just scoffed at the idea that people could use simple tools to block stress and boost positive emotions. Their sentiment was, "Right! People are going to use mental practices to rewire their emotional brains to process stress effectively? They are going to be conscious? There's a laugh! People just aren't that disciplined. We've got them just where we want them, believing that our little silver bullets are their saviors."

A Matter of Responsibility

Then a little time passed and the method began to catch on enough that the drug companies assigned "the EBT problem" to their social responsibility committee. The committee agreed to fund a grant for $25,000 to offer to the nonprofit organization that had developed the tools, a wise move for public relations. But after a few conference calls between the social responsibility committee and the directors of the small institute (really a small band of therapists and researchers who were keen on the method), the whole plan fell apart. The small but determined nonprofit organization politely passed on the funds.

A year passed, and some of the drug company's shareholders questioned them about the grant. In short order, George, the CEO, a walrus of a man in his early 40s who was looking to make his mark, got the idea to buy the EBT method. They would negotiate a deal, and perhaps it would cost them $1 million, but it would be great for public relations. Once they owned the method—including the pending patent rights for the tools, they would move slowly through legal processes and have it reviewed by their pack of attorneys. They would have no choice but to remove EBT from the market since the emotional brain was largely uncharted territory. Then who knew how long it would take to thoroughly assess the risks involved? It could take decades!

So George sent his top attorney, Marvin Dodd, a man he could always count on when he had problems with shareholders, to San Francisco to talk with the EBT people and secure the purchase. It turned out to be a quick jaunt for Marvin, and he came back to George with a recommendation against the purchase. The nonprofit company was small and not well organized, so he concluded that they weren't a real threat to their business.

Right about that time, a mid-level actress started using the EBT and lost 30 pounds, as well as her yen for vodka, and reclaimed her radiant look—the one that had paved her way to success. She did the normal thing and posed for a short piece in a magazine. It wasn't a cover shot but one near the back of the magazine—the stories readers don't pay much attention to. A bit later, the magazine's annual issue hit the newsstands: follow-up stories of people previously featured by the magazine who had sworn off sugar, alcohol, or cigarettes, or cut up their credit cards the year before. Instead of lapses in these promises, as would be expected, the year passed and the star was still lean, clean, and sober. The photo of her even seemed free of airbrushing, and her smile seemed authentic, not forced. In fact, there appeared to be a look of peace on her face. The little organization that taught EBT had double the number of hits on its Website during the week the issue was on the stands.

Soon, faith-based organizations caught on to the method, opening up space in their basements and their unused rooms. They figured, why not take a chance and see what these little tools can do? After all, the emotional brain is the seat of the soul. Then, a few charter schools started teaching the tools to students, and their academic scores improved, and the bullying in the playground seemed to stop. Furthermore, the children went home and the parents had no idea why they were so well behaved. No temper tantrums. No discipline problems. In fact, when the parents flipped out after a ridiculously stressful day at work, it was the kids who seemed to take on the parent role. They calmed their parents down, letting them know that they didn't have to be perfect to be wonderful, and reassuring them that this moment of stress was just the state of the emotional brain and would soon pass.

A Speck of Dust in a Sandstorm

Still all this interest was like a speck of dust in a sandstorm to the drug companies, who knew they had the goods. They had the knock-out drops for sleeping, the ramrod meds to treat mood, and the magical pill that blocked fat absorption, so that you could still eat fatty, unhealthy food and try to lose weight by excreting the fat. In their sales meetings, they stuck with their rationale that the public was too daft to differentiate between pills they really needed and ones that treated stress-related conditions that could be cured with a walk around the block, a healthy diet, a good night's sleep, and a little emotional brain training.

Things didn't get shaken up until George convened a staff meeting one January to discuss reduced profits. In attendance were George, a clutch of lawyers, two women from the social responsibility committee, and Marvin, the attorney that George had sent off to explore buying the method a few years before.

The meeting got off to an unfortunate start. It might have been that stagnant air but George had this gnawing feeling, the cooped up sense you get when you're stuck. Florence, from the social responsibility committee, watched George start jiggling his right leg. She knew that was a bad sign.

Then he began tapping his pencil on the conference table. Something was wrong with George, she thought. Maybe he had had a bad night drinking the evening before. Perhaps his wife, Kate, was on one of her spending rampages, or his mid-20s daughter, Alice had finally contacted him again and was acting out. Who really knew?

Mirror Neurons Chattering

Actually, what was bothering George was right in the room. Nothing was overtly wrong, but he could sense that something was different, and this made him feel uneasy. This sense came from the work of a special type of neuron, called a *mirror neuron.* Neurons are nerve cells that send and receive electrical or chemical signals to transmit information through the body. The specialized mirror neurons (the ones that were being activated to make George feel uneasy) pick up signals not from an external stimulus, but from the internal state of another person or animal nearby. The mirror neurons then replicate this state within you, providing accurate information so you can determine whether an approaching stranger is friend or foe. Think of mirror neurons as a universal sensing system that evolved over the millennia to ensure the survival of the species.

At this moment, George's mirror neurons were chattering away, having instantly picked up signals in the room that something was different. In the world of brain chemistry, "different" translates to "bad," as the brain prefers everything to stay the same. It prefers monotony, a throwback to new foods being more apt to be poisonous and new people more apt to be foes (complete with bows, arrows, sticks, or stones to do us in). George's mirror neurons were picking up danger.

George was accustomed to showing up at the meeting, scanning the room, and sensing the familiar group of employees: Stan with his quirky smile and Julie, with laptop open, lost in thought. Florence was there, too, chatting with others who were arriving, relaxed, and yet well controlled. This time, though, he sensed that something was amiss. He had a sudden urge to open the windows, as if he needed a breath of fresh air. Of course he knew that the windows were sealed and air was coming into the room through the return, yet he felt closed in. George furrowed his brows and tried to figure out what was wrong with him, and then he spotted Marvin, his drinking buddy and a veteran of 19 years of corporate law, the lynchpin of the team that had gotten their last drug through the FDA. He was the guy who had nixed the purchase of the little nonprofit organization that developed those stress tools—what was it called? EB something.

Since the holidays, he hadn't seen much of Marvin, who had been immersed in the legal issues around an application to the FDA. At that moment, George recognized the problem: something was different about Marvin. He couldn't quite pin it down. The mirror neurons he relied on to feel safe, knowing that his emotional connection with others was the same (even though not all that great), were chattering. Something was definitely off.

It was Marvin. What was wrong with him anyway? He looked so damn calm. George didn't need a top attorney who was calm. He needed a steely determination to get drugs pushed through the Feds. Maybe Marvin was just having an off day (the first day back from a trip to Tahiti), or maybe he had taken a course in Tibetan meditation. That couldn't be. Marvin wasn't the type to meditate.

Perhaps it was his new girlfriend. Wasn't she a plastic surgeon? Perhaps he had gotten some freshening up, a little nip or tuck or one of those new "power facials" men were getting. George decided to start the meeting and just barrel ahead, as there was a long list of agenda items. But the more he talked, the worse he felt.

The room was hot, and his words weren't making sense. It seemed like nobody was really listening to him, and he hated that feeling. He felt a little dizzy. His heart problem was getting to him. And then all of a sudden, George snapped. He threw his pencil across the table, and said in a deep growl, "Nobody's listening to me . . . and damn it, Marvin, what's wrong with you?"

Marvin looked back at George. He had never seen George flip out in a board meeting. He didn't say anything, but instead just pondered what could be going on with his friend. George's ears got redder, and all eyes turned to George. He said to Marvin, "Something is different about you."

Marvin looked right in his friend's eyes, and said, "I know."

The room was still. And then George said, "Well, what is it?"

Marvin took in George's gaze, knowing that his buddy, and boss, was out on a limb. He shrugged and slipped down in his chair, in an effort to lessen the tension, and said, "It's that stress thing we tried to buy out."

George's face dropped. He thought, *Great, my top attorney has joined a cult.*

Marvin said, "My son was caught smoking marijuana, and my girlfriend couldn't sleep at night, and I was getting a paunch, so, I decided to try it. It's a stress thing. You switch your brain so that you feel good. Now I feel better; in fact, I feel great."

George said nothing, though he was a little curious. His mind wandered, searching for an explanation that made sense. Then he got it. He laughed to himself. Of course he knew what was going on. Marvin had started drinking again. No wonder he was peaceful. Who isn't quiet when they are hungover?

George cleared his throat, looked down at the memo with the agenda items carefully listed, and noticed his pencil on the floor at his feet. Just as he opened his mouth to address the first agenda item, he carefully placed the heel of his wing tip on the pencil and dug in. The pencil snapped, and the noise echoed around the room.

Then George continued the meeting.

A Team Player

Four years and seven days later, George was standing in front of the company's building, with Florence right by his side. Before them was an oblong folding table, covered with a green tablecloth and plates of cookies and assorted cakes. Even upper management had pitched in to make the day of fundraising a success, rising early in the morning to bake banana bread or to bring slice-and-bake cookies. Florence was shuffling cakes around on the table, putting the most expensive ones at the front, to improve the chance that, as employees passed the table on their way back into the building, they would buy the baked items.

Public demand for their various medications had fallen off so much that throwing a bake sale made it onto the list of financial stabilizing strategies that George was implementing. As EBT had caught on, the need for medication plummeted. EBT was being used by the military, and also by colleges that were teaching it to students as they entered their freshman year. Therapists now taught the tools routinely, and in the popular press, stories of the power of the emotional brain appeared on the same page as the stories of various international skirmishes or global warming. In fact, the five tools were on milk containers, and nearly everyone had a mobile device to check in and use the tools to switch their brains back to well-being whenever they hit with the aggravations of daily life. Doctors had also begun teaching healthy lifestyles and, with their patients' brains in balance, and the toxic chemical cascade of stress hormones no longer driving them to extremes, it wasn't hard for them to eat healthily, sleep well, and go to the gym. Medical researchers could actually focus on diseases not caused by stress, and medications for symptom relief were much less widely used. Having medicine cabinets full of those extra designer drugs for stress symptoms seemed to have gone the way of soda cans, shopping bags, and those inch-thick T-bone steaks with that ribbon of fat all around. Popping pills seemed old-fashioned, too, but not so out of fashion as to become retro and chic.

So with the company's profits in the tank and more stockholders giving up on them, George decided on bake sales. It was a way to show a positive attitude and to make ends meet. And George was leading the way for his company that day, standing in front of his building with his cash box, sorting the nickels from the dimes. After all, he had to make change for the employees who bought the big-ticket items, the $10.45 coconut topped cakes, and, on a really good day, they could sell out of the $13.50 sheet cakes. Oh well, it kept the doors of the company open until he could figure out his next step.

The Last Pencil

As George was writing out a receipt for the woman who was buying the sheet cake, he dropped his pencil and it fell to the pavement. He looked down at the pencil and realized that he was of mind to step on it. He loved stepping on pencils, even more now because his blood pressure was up, he had put on weight, and he felt right on the edge. It was so satisfying to crush that pencil and hear it snap.

Yet the sight of the pencil triggered the memory of that day in the boardroom with Marvin, who was no longer with the company. Marvin had left to set up a nonprofit for legal services to help those who had been injured by medication misuse. And rumor was he was happy. Just thinking about Marvin's peacefulness caused George feel a wave of calmness in his chest. Perhaps Marvin hadn't been drinking after all. In fact, just for an instant George thought, *That peacefulness, or joy, or whatever it was that Marvin got. Maybe, just maybe, I could get it, too.*

Then George reached down, picked up the pencil, and tucked it into his pocket.

Chapter 2

Brain Basics

The brain is the central command post of your being, orchestrating your survival. It has various parts, all of which are good for some things, but not others. For example, the neocortex—the lofty center of consciousness as well as of moment-to-moment planning and deciding—is good at analyzing and weighing options, while the reptilian brain, which marshals the launch of the fight-or-flight response, is good at quick decisions based on previous experience. So different parts of the brain are dominant during different situations. The brain constantly has to gauge the level of threat to figure out which part of the brain should run the show at a particular time. If you were being chased by a lion, the thinking brain would be of little use with its slow decision-making process, so the primitive, reflexive brain would be triggered.

Understanding how these areas—plus the emotional mammalian, or limbic brain—operate is essential to identifying your brain state and using the tools to switch from stress to joy.

THE REPTILE WITHIN (THE BRAIN STEM)

The most primitive area of the brain is the smallest, the oldest, and the quickest. Sitting at the base of the skull, it is quite similar to the entire brain of a reptile. It determines your level of alertness and is the home base of the fight-or-flight response. The reptilian brain, or the brain stem, reacts very quickly, so that, if a lion is chasing you, you don't sit around wondering what kind of lion it is or sharing a few choice words with it. You just escape. You run for the cave and save your life. It is also the role of the reptilian brain to orchestrate changes in basic bodily processes like respiration, blood pressure, and heart rate.

The trouble with the reptilian brain is that, because there aren't a lot of lions roaming into your village these days, it is often a loose cannon, firing but not very accurately. Like a snake, it is snappish. When the reptilian brain is aroused, it tends to err on the side of negativity, perpetually overestimating threats. It always bets on the worst-case scenario, a trait that is perfectly designed to keep your hunter-gatherer ancestors alive but isn't very helpful today.

The reptilian brain never made the leap to the 21st century. It can't nicely tease apart varying levels of threat is neat packages. Rather, it sees every change from the status quo as a hungry rampaging lion. And these stresses can come from any number of places. New experience? That's psychological stress. Go on a diet? That's metabolic stress. Rage at the driver who stole your parking space? That's emotional stress. Each of these types of stress is shunted into the reptilian brain as if your life were on the line. In fact, it sees lions everywhere, and what's more, it mixes these three kinds of stress together, so the minor backache, the food hangover, and a partner's crabby mood add up to one major bundle of stress that triggers the reptilian brain, putting it in charge. What's more, a stressor in real time stirs up all past incantations of the experience, so the stress of your current boss's glare stirs memories of disapproving stares of every authority figure in your past, amplifying your stress. So, you have no idea why you feel so bad. You just do.

You're dealing with illogic here, so even though the world seems crazy at times, the equipment you have to deal with it is as bad or worse. This is not what "those people" have but what everyone has, and what is triggered, given enough stress. When the reptilian brain is triggered, moderation is not in its repertoire. It pulls out the stops, because the overriding message is that you are in extreme danger. And you know that you must do whatever it takes to protect yourself—to get back to that comfortable place where your brain feels safe.

Let's say you go on a diet, causing metabolic stress, and then you mix this with other stressors in your life. You know you're trying to eat healthy, but in a flash all you want is those chocolate cupcakes at the convenience store, the ones with the white squiggles on top, and before you know it you're in the car racing to the store. You're going to get what you want when you want it. The reptilian brain is triggered! Then you blame yourself for having no willpower, but you can't fight that survival drive. What about when a meeting gets really tense? When you can't stand sitting there for another minute, that sense that you will do whatever it takes to get out of that room comes from the activation of the reptilian brain. Of course you'll stomp out of the meeting or tell a white lie to make a quick exit. Who wouldn't when a lion was chasing them? Throw the keys across the room, and rant and rave for a while? That's a survival response and rather tame, really, compared to the violence that could occur when battling off that lion.

To make matters worse, when the reptilian brain is aroused, there is an immediate time warp. You can't see around the bend to a different tomorrow or reflect back on yesterday to see how different it was from this rotten situation you find yourself in now. To assure that you will do whatever it takes to survive, your brain tricks you into perceiving that there is only now. It always has been this dire, and it always will be this dire. No reflecting on or anticipating a better situation. Instead, you are consumed by your terror and feel overwhelmed, lost, and open to doing whatever it takes to alleviate your pain.

When your reptilian brain is in charge, you strive for comfort and safety in whatever way is possible. You boost your mood to high intensity well-being through hedonic rewards, or pleasure for pleasure's sake. The feeling of pleasure you get through hedonic rewards is all based on creating certain neurotransmitters—the chemicals that relay messages from neuron to neuron. Hedonic rewards generate a blast of the feel-good neurotransmitters, including dopamine, oxytocin, serotonin, and endorphins. These positive neurotransmitters are produced when the body senses that you are doing something that aids in your survival. For example, you grab for the chocolate because that provides a lot of calories. Because your body needs calories to survive, it is programmed to think that calories are good. So it gives you a burst of pleasure.

Although hedonic pleasures can be part of a life well lived, the repeated use of them can be dangerous and lead to addiction by creating unnatural highs and lows, as well as an imbalance in your neurotransmitters. Once the brain is sensitized to these rewards, the driver for cravings becomes the desire to balance the neurotransmitters—in other words, to combat the lows with highs. The stress-induced reward-deficiency syndrome does not take no for an answer, and does whatever it takes to feel that relief and satisfaction.

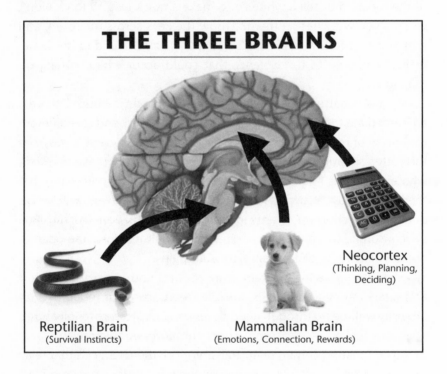

THE THREE BRAINS

Neocortex
(Thinking, Planning, Deciding)

Reptilian Brain
(Survival Instincts)

Mammalian Brain
(Emotions, Connection, Rewards)

THE CUDDLY PUPPY (THE LIMBIC BRAIN)

If the reptilian brain is the snappish reptile, the mammalian brain, or limbic brain, is the cuddly puppy. It is this area of the brain that thrives on connection, and without a limbic brain, mothers would not care for their young. When researchers attach electrodes to study the functions of the various regions of the brain, it is always the limbic brain that comes out as the emotional core of our being.

Your limbic brain is the seat of emotional balance, relationship intimacy, spiritual connection, and pleasure. How you connect with yourself, others, and life is largely determined by the state of your emotional brain.

As a culture that values mind over matter and thoughts over feelings, emotions take a backseat. Yet emotions are important because they are the genetically determined best way for you to know what you really need—so that you can take care of it and avoid experiencing ramped up stress levels.

The limbic brain is the clearinghouse for all the stress that pours in through your senses, and it acts as the first step in stress processing. It sorts though vastly different kinds of information—the thoughts, emotional memories, unconscious expectations, and body messages—analyzing and prioritizing it, and then adroitly chooses the most important need, and sends up a message in the form of an emotion to the neocortical brain. The most amazing processor on the planet, the limbic brain spontaneously titrates the strength of the message based on the importance of the need.

Yet as you shall see, accessing that information and interpreting it accurately is wired into the brain—or not—principally by your early experiences. Before adolescence, you're apt to be sensitive to the emotional brain because you have no formidable thinking brain, or neocortex, to distract your attention from your emotions. Once puberty passes, the neocortex becomes more dominant, and instead of being astonishingly intuitive, as children are, you process daily life by trying to figure things out. That can work well only if each thought pulsates with an emotional core, so you don't lose track of that essential information.

Yet in times of stress, the emotions go on the fritz, and you enter into *hyperarousal,* in which emotions overwhelm, or *dissociation,* in which you lose the ability to feel. Both impact the thinking processes. You're lost in your thoughts, ruminating, overanalyzing everything to give you the illusion of control. Or you become oddly mindless, forgetful, and blanked out. That fight you had with your partner never existed. The agreement you made to show up on time? Who remembers that? You've lost your security. You are no longer grounded in your emotions.

Our Earliest Wiring

The adaptability of the human brain is astonishing, with experience shaping its responsiveness so that a particular brain is better suited to the environment in which it is born. Although the reptilian brain is largely formed at birth, the limbic brain develops primarily in the last trimester of pregnancy and the first few years of life. Early on it is like a sponge, soaking in the environment so it can best support survival.

Yet this early programming is quite individual, and even intimate, because the organ of transmission is the parent's own limbic brain. In the best of all worlds, the parent is balanced, capable of moving through stress and back to that sweet spot of joy. If so, the parent can read the inner state of the child and determine what the child needs, given that the child's neocortex is not developed enough to do this on its own. The parent, regardless of which brain state he or she is in, can then find the quickest, easiest pathway back to well-being for the child.

The best chance that the child will become wired for resilience and joy is that the parent is resilient and in joy. In this secure attachment between parent and child, the child downloads the parent's circuits of reading his or her emotional state. The child learns to stay consistently tuned into emotions and to read them accurately, thus developing a secure emotional attachment to self.

This vulnerable period of early imprinting of how the infant processes stress is important because while a brain area is developing, memories are strongly encoded. In the first year of life, emotional connection is key, and in the second year of life, parents who have succeeded in emotionally connecting with their children need to draw on their skills of setting limits, not being permissive or depriving.

The first few years of parenting are more than challenging, and this is in part because the way of connecting with a child originates in your unconscious memory system. Just when you thought you were nothing like your parents, everything you say sounds *just like them*. It's almost as if you have been invaded. The attachment style is passed from parent to child with a 70 percent transmission rate. A small tendency to distance or merge, to be too hard or too soft, to be excessively rigid or impossibly chaotic shows up in your facial expression, your touch, your words, just as it did your parents' attachment style. I remember a *Mad* magazine comic in which the straight parents raise hippie children who raise straight kids. If you do not rewire your own unconscious memory system for secure attachment, chances are that your children will copy your own form of insecure attachment or follow another one that is equally insecure.

In the best of all worlds, in those countless interactions that shape the emotional architecture of your brain, the parent installs: 1) a secure attachment to self that offers a sanctuary within, a safe place to return to when all else fails or just because it feels good; 2) the tools of resiliency, those tracks in the brain that lead back to joy no matter what the immediate brain state; and 3) basic expectations about life that are reasonable, clear, and flexible, stored in the unconscious memory so that even when you don't know what you're doing, there is a safety net of adaptive thoughts that nudge you forward.

The Elusive Unconscious Mind

The fact that all this brain programming is going on is pretty scary. It would not be nearly as frightening if it were conscious, if you could map out what you know and don't know, and then set about filling in the holes of your learning. However, the functioning of the limbic brain is so core to survival that your genes do not leave it to the vicissitudes of conscious thought. What if you had a memory lapse? What if you took a day off from being conscious?

There are two kinds of memory—conscious and unconscious. Conscious memory is what you know you know—the stories you tell, the dates you remember, the analysis you do. It is stored mainly in the thinking brain, or the neocortex. Unconscious memory, on the other hand is stored primarily in the emotional brain. It is what you don't know you know—that gut feeling that something is wrong, that wordless knowing that someone is trustworthy, the unconscious expectation that you don't matter. Conscious memory is controllable to some extent: you decide to learn a new computer program, or about weather forecasting, or how to arrange flowers. Unconscious memory, on the other hand, is not within your control. It doesn't allow you to pick and choose your memories of daily life. Instead, all your experiences flood into the unconscious mind, and the ones stored during stress may be particularly misleading. Beliefs such as the fact that you aren't good enough or the certainty that men will always leave you are stored in your unconscious mind. If asked point blank if you believed that, you'd quite honestly say that it's hogwash, even if, in fact, those emotional memories shaped every one of your choices in that arena.

All these unconscious memories are based on an influx of information into your limbic brain—20 million pieces per second compared to a paltry 40 pieces for your conscious memory housed in the neocortex. And these memories are stored in survival-based vaults in your mind, creating a set of basic beliefs about your condition that can easily trump conscious thought. For example, let's say a young woman is repeatedly treated by her parents as if she is a princess and that the rules of life do not apply to her. Locked into her unconscious mind is a basic expectation of which she is not aware: that the world owes her. Or take another child, and no matter how loving, smart, and successful a child is, the repeated contact of the parent's own unconscious memory of not being worthy is passed along to him. No matter how many advanced degrees he earns, there is still in his gut a feeling of unease, as if at any moment he would be found out and labeled an imposter.

What's particularly pernicious about these emotional memories of how to process stress, of the secure or insecure connection with yourself and your basic expectations of life, is that you would swear on a stack of Bibles that you are not impacted by them. When you arouse a conscious memory, you can tell you are digging up information previously stored. Searching to remember a sister-in-law's birthday and then, bingo, it's January 7. Great! I remembered that. With emotional memory, there is no *source attribution* or sense that whatever is happening right now is not just about the current moment, that something from the past is actively infiltrating the experience. With emotional memory, when see your friend wrinkle her nose, that information leaps into the emotional brain, arouses every last memory from every similar nose-wrinkling experience—most of which involve a nose wrinkling in disgust and rejection. And when you find out that your friend is having an allergy attack, not rejecting you, it's too late. The unconscious memories of the past have amplified your stress and before she can reach for a tissue, it's World War III.

This is why much of EBT focuses on rewiring those unconscious circuits, using the emotions of your limbic brain to track down those memories, bring them to the attention of the neocortical mind, and burn into your circuits' memories that are adaptive. These new circuits usher you safety through stresses and keep you from overreacting, from being afraid of another emotional bomb going off when you least expect it. This is also why we love stress in EBT, because in stress these emotional memories are accessible for the adroit rewiring by using the tools; in other words, the pathway to emotional freedom is the through the portal of emotions during stress, and not something that can be accomplished by insights and positive thoughts alone.

The Analyzer (the Neocortex)

Last but not least is the neocortex—the thinking brain—which evolves last in life. The neocortex is revered because it is the most complex part of the brain, which can think abstract thoughts, analyze information effectively, and make stellar decisions.

With EBT, you will use the power of the prefrontal cortex—a part of the neocortex that is located just behind the eyebrows—to rewire your emotional circuitry. One of the most important attributes of the prefrontal cortex is consciousness and the capacity to choose rewards.

Your brain is reward driven, so every choice you make is based on rewards, even if the choices are completely unconscious. Using the tools makes you aware of your choices.

The prefrontal cortex is the grand overseer of the emotional brain. And when it is not stressed, it functions magnificently, providing the emotional brain with the repeated experiences it needs to feel a secure attachment, a sanctuary within, the tools of resilience, and the most basic expectations that bring safety and power. It can also appraise your emotional state and do what needs to be done to process the stresses of your current situation back to joy.

But what about really bad situations in which there seems to be no good option? Or what about the situation where the best choice is to tolerate it instead of resolving it? Even in these situations, the prefrontal cortex can clear away the stress in the emotional brain, so that it can choose between shades of gray and hold on tight even when taking no action is the most challenging thing. With enough attention and focus and a few powerful tools, the prefrontal cortex can analyze the unconscious expectations in the emotional brain and break free from the ones that don't conform to its authentic needs and values. It can find meaning in life, and see even rotten situations that would otherwise lead to teeth clenching and feeling constantly on edge. And it can arouse the moral centers in the brain to imbue any situation with higher meaning, causing an intense rush of feel-good neurotransmitters that swamp the pain.

When the neocortex that is not in stress is dominant and in charge, you can aim for positive emotions not through the hedonic rewards but through eudonic rewards. These are the rewards you get when you bring blueberry muffins to the sick neighbor or hold your tongue instead of telling someone I told you so. It is the reward of being good, of being of higher purpose, and of spirit instead of ego.

Eudonic pleasures are produced because there are strong connections between the conscious thought of the neocortical brain and the moral and reward centers of the emotional brain—the combination of the limbic brain and the reptilian brain. Doing something meaningful—even just the thought of being good—

awakens the pleasure centers of the brain, sending ripples of joy through your body. You might say that you are naturally built to do unto others as you would have them do unto you. It is woven into your psyche, because without that capacity to share resources during times of need, the species would not have survived.

What's more, eudonic rewards are not easily sated. Instead of the brain adapting to them so that, in time, we are like rats on a wheel wanting more and more, the brain continues to produce feel-good neurotransmitters in response to these pleasures for life. Unlike hedonic reward, eudonic rewards do not easily lead to compulsive and addictive behavior.

PUTTING THEM ALL TOGETHER

Despite the separate structures and functions of the three brains, the neurological goal of most therapies is neural integration; that is, the smooth communications between all parts of the brain and their working together in a cohesive and effective way. How each area of the brain functions, and how they chatter and cooperate as a unified whole, is largely a matter of how they are wired. In Chapter 3, you'll see how that wiring forms, and how different kinds of wires take different routes through the brain.

A Perky Woman in a Smart Suit

Imagine this: A year after the pharmaceutical company bake sale, I was giving a talk at the San Francisco Bay Club, a posh exercise palace for well-heeled young professionals and the urban fitness crowd. A perky woman in a smart suit and designer shoes came up to the podium afterward.

She said, "My husband needs these tools. Or rather, I need my husband to get these tools. He is driving me crazy, and I'm so worried about him. He is a bundle of nerves, and his blood pressure is off the charts. He obsesses about his bloating and indigestion, and he spends hours in the bathroom. At night he paces the floor or he hits the bed, and then he snores so loudly that I can't sleep."

She adjusted her huge leather bag on her shoulder, and then crossed her arms over her chest.

"He had the top job for a pharmaceutical company, a huge salary, and stock options, and three months ago they dumped him. He was out on the street."

I looked into her eyes and sighed. *How sad,* I thought.

"Before that, I had a life. In the morning I worked out, and then I went to lunch with friends. I played tennis in the afternoons, went shopping, collected antiques, and went to the symphony. I loved my husband, but I have no idea where that man went.

"Now I'm living with a control freak who micromanages my time, wants me there to do everything for him, and holes himself away in the den, eating tons of candy, popping antacids, drinking, and playing video games.

"I am miserable and stressed. I want my life back. Help!"

My chest felt tight just listening to her, no doubt her desperation traveling (via the mirror neuron route) into the recesses of my own emotional brain. I took a deep breath, exhaled, and said, "I'm sorry you're going through this. Anyone in the family who uses the tools affects everyone else. Emotions are catching."

Her eyes widened, and she said, "Are you kidding? I've already signed up. I'm getting the skills, but you just don't know. This stress has dumped emotional toxins all though my house. It's not a home. It's a prison. I don't even like going there."

Then her shoulders sank, her perky look turned sad. "Oh what's the use? He'll never pry himself out of the den for long enough to learn the tools."

"Does he have an iPhone?" I asked.

"He has a love affair with his iPhone. He strokes his iPhone. He has the perfect, semi-soft, charcoal-toned case for his iPhone."

I shrugged, "There's an EBT application of the tools. He can try it out that way. If he likes it and wants to see me for one-on-one coaching, I'll be happy to see him."

"Perfect!" she said. "My name is Kate Samuels. My husband is George. You'll be hearing from us."

And with that, she turned briskly, and left the room.

What George Most Wanted

Two weeks later, George arrived in my office, and at once I was struck by what a larger than life man he was. He was big and barrel-chested, with a shock of dark hair, longer than most executives wear, and he seemed like a man on a mission.

"How may I be of help?" I asked.

George reached in his pocket and pulled out a brown paper sack and emptied its contents onto my desk. Tan plastic pill bottles with white tops spilled out, cellophane slabs of pink chewable pills, along with an assortment of heat patches, suppositories, stool softeners, and what looked like a blood pressure medication, blood sugar drugs, antidepressants, and sleeping pills came spilling out.

George started sorting through the pills, but then stopped, grabbed the whole pile of them, and said, "I am here for revenge . . . money . . . integrity. Do you see this? These pills are costing me an arm and a leg. When my company was on its way down, I changed everyone's health insurance policy to a high deductible. Now it's costing me $24.43 per day to take these pills.

"Can you believe what those guys did to me? After 19 years of service, I can't afford to take the lousy medications I need, because of the stress my job caused me. I gave them my life. I missed out on my family all those years. I'm stopping these damn pills if it's the last thing I do."

George's face was bright red and he looked like he was going to blow a blood vessel. Then a slight mist came over his eyes and George shook his head and said, "I even threw a bake sale for them."

George sighed, and slowly began gathering up the pill bottles, and putting them back into his brown paper bag, and tucked them in the pocket of his jacket.

I felt sad just listening to him.

"And that's not the half of it . . . my basement has been turned into a storehouse for my wife's objects of blatant overspending. She leaves in the morning, even though I need her. She goes to the gym, and then stops off and pays $4 for a latte without thinking about my stress or financial crisis. Then it's off to scavenging to every mall, roadside antique store, or even . . . garage sale. Laurel, she is totally out of control!"

I sighed, nodded, and said, "Tell me more."

George got up from the chair, and he started pacing around the office. "Then there's my daughter." He looked at me again, seeming to size me up to see if he trusted me with the bombshell he was about to unload.

"I never thought Kate and I were perfect parents, but our one and only child, Alice—she has now changed her name to Ace—was a happy little girl. She was the light of our lives, and we gave her everything she wanted. We worried about her every step; from whether she should take piano or violin to which of the private schools best fit for her talents. We did everything we could to make her life successful, and to make her happy."

George stopped pacing and sat down on the chair.

"We paid for her to go to a small liberal arts college at $50 grand per year, and after five years, she hadn't figured out her major, and never even gave us the courtesy of graduating.

"Then she disappeared. She stopped contacting us, except to set off a few emotional land mines, saying that she felt suffocated by us, and that we were controlling. She said we made her feel bad about herself."

"How sad," I said, feeling a wave of sorrow in my body.

"Then last night she arrived on our doorstep with her new boyfriend, whom we don't know, not to mention that Ace is now five months pregnant with the child of her old boyfriend who was arrested for selling oxycontin to college kids and was sent to the slammer. What does my daughter want? A handout? No, she wants to live with us. She wants to mend fences, she and her lover, Squeaky, some scrawny mountain biker guy. They showed up together. They both look like they have very large appetites.

George paused, then, leaning toward me, eyes like saucers, he said, "Can you imagine that she would do this to me? I had the immediate urge to get in my Porsche, start driving, and never come back. It took me a minute to realize that my car had been repossessed."

With that George slumped back into his chair and sighed, "I am stuck. I am totally and completely stuck."

I shook my head, and said, "How perfect."

A Moment of Opportunity

George's face turned slightly red, but he tolerated the irritation and waited for what came next.

"First of all, I'm glad to know what is bothering you, but EBT is not talk therapy. It's brain training. We like stress in this training because it provides a moment of opportunity. Each stressful event in your life is perfect, because if you use the tools when in stress, the wires of your emotional circuitry are open to remodeling. Each upset is just a way to find a wire that is causing you stress and then rewire it, essentially nipping it in the bud.

"If we work together, you will need medical management. You'll need to go to your physician every three months to adjust your medications. You don't go cold turkey, but wait for the tools to do their job and, as they do the need for them will diminish."

"That's fair enough."

"Are you getting much exercise?"

He looked sheepish. "No, not much."

"What about healthy food: fruits, vegetables, lean protein?"

He said nothing.

"And sleep—eight hours in bed, no more than ten?"

George said nothing.

"Start cleaning up your lifestyle and working closely with your physician. We don't want the extra stress caused by avoiding those changes."

He nodded, "I can do that."

"You are embarking on a training that will transform your life. The tools are simple, but not easy, and they are extremely powerful. You will not focus on what is wrong with your life or what stresses you face. Instead you will focus on your wiring—the pathways in your brain that determine how you process daily life. Some wires work well, moving you through a stressful situation with equanimity and dropping you off back in a state of feeling great. Other wires drop you into a black hole of stress, and you feel confused, overwhelmed and lost."

"That's me."

"When you feel awful, instead of analyzing what is wrong with you, beating yourself up for not getting it right, or blaming your wife, daughter or . . ."

"Squeaky."

". . . blaming Squeaky for your problem, you put the blame where it belongs: on your wiring. Then you use a tool to rewire it."

"Sounds good to me. Okay, sign me up."

Chapter 3

It's Just a Wire!

Every response you have in daily life is just the triggering of a wire. When the alarm goes off in the morning, and you respond by shutting it off, rolling over, and going back to sleep, that's a wire. When you come home from work, make a beeline to the refrigerator, and reach for that leftover poached salmon and rosemary potatoes, that's a wire, too.

In fact, every one of our emotions, thoughts, and actions is a wire, a string of nerve cells or neurons that link together in a particular pattern. Each person has about 100 billion neurons, and each one connects with 100 to 100,000 others, to create wires, or circuits. They are the basis for all learning; that is, carrying forward the experiences of the past so that our responses to the current moment and the plans for the future are adaptive and keep us in the game of life.

THINKING IN TERMS OF WIRES

So what actually happens when a wire is triggered? Let's say the alarm sounds, and a stimulus enters the brain. The brain's first order of business is to look for a past experience that is similar to what it has just sensed. It looks for an existing wire to trigger because triggering an already existing wire is the easiest option. If the brain finds one similar enough to an experience that occurred before, it arouses an old wire. But what if you had never had an alarm? What if, while growing up, your mother always gently awakened you when it was time? If this was the case, the brain could lay down a fresh new circuit, but it much prefers to use already formed wires rather than create new ones. Ring bells in the morning, not the familiar buzzer of an alarm, and it will happily trigger the buzzer alarm circuit. It leaves off the nuance of the current experience, and in many ways, this desensitizes us to the vibrant complexity and freshness of the current moment. As we age, we funnel more and more of the crazy, delightful, enthralling new things that occur into old circuits, and more and more everything looks the same, even when it is not.

When a circuit is triggered, neurons that were on their own, not linked at all, instantly snap into place with other neurons in a familiar pattern. You know the drill. You interpret that wire as, *Time to get up!* Once your feet are on the floor and you're off to take that hot shower or check the morning news, that circuit quiets down—the activation of those neurons peters out. Left behind is *a memory trace,* a slight tendency for those very same neurons to connect in response to the same or similar stimulus, in the very same pattern again. That enables you to move experiences forward and make presumably better decisions that are informed by the past.

But not all memory traces are alike. The more often a circuit is aroused, the stronger it becomes; in essence, neurons that fire together wire together. So some circuits are like thin silk threads and others are like thick bristly ropes. Other things that cause wires to strengthen are highly emotional experiences. Because emotion indicates a response to a need and meeting needs is the basis for survival, a more emotional experience is remembered preferentially. The memory trace is strong. The same goes for repeated experiences—habits. It's convenient to have repetition increase the strength of the connection, so you don't have to think about filling up the coffee mug and putting it next to you in the car on your drive to work. That wire has been activated so many times that it is strong, like rope.

And what about trauma—really dangerous moments? Those threat-to-survival moments encode a circuit instantly that rumbles within you for life, fully encoded in the worry circuit in the brain. Even a slight stimulus that resembles that traumatic experience—the smell of the tanks, the heightened heart rate, the eerie silence on a dark night—triggers a memory from the backfield of the mind, and you're in a panic. The power you have is to be the overseer of these circuits, because the more you arouse them, the stronger the traces will be and in a use-it-or-lose-it principle, and the more you don't fire it, the more it will dissemble, lose that trace, and fall away.

It's Not Me—It's My Wiring!

All wires that enable you to self-regulate—to meet the stresses of the day and make those small but important adjustments to survive and thrive—have three phases: emotional processing, neocortical processing, and corrective action. And the brain responds in a split second with the whole wire—not just one part of it—and that electrical and chemical pathway in your brain shapes your responses to life. If you walk into a room and flip on the light switch, the overhead light turns on. If you wanted a different result, say for the table lamp to turn on instead of the overhead light, you'd have to rewire that switch.

That's what you are doing with these five tools; you're rewiring your switches. It takes a while to start thinking in terms of wires, but as you read this book, I hope you start to think along these lines. I also hope you will be aware of the other ways you try to create change, what your mode of stress processing is now and why many of them soothe you but don't rewire, so you don't change. Talking about and sharing problems, for instance, is a popular way people try to deal with stress. Unfortunately, with this method, the wires are still in the wall; you're just talking about why that table light won't go on instead of the overhead light.

So, for example, is this woman wiring a new circuit—creating transformation—or just retreading the old? "My husband is really bothering me. We have issues, and we just avoid talking about them because I know he brings up my fear of abandonment when he works

39

late, and he knows that when I start to give him any advice, he thinks I'm being shrill, and then his mind shuts off and he doesn't listen to me. Then I feel like I could be violent because I wasn't listened to as a little girl, and nobody ever listens to me, especially my husband. Which means that I lose my interest in romance, and then he becomes demanding and pouts, both of which are a huge turnoff for me, so what can I do?"

No wiring change. She soothed, comforted, and distracted herself, but no circuit changed; in fact, she strengthened the circuit of thinking about her distress and analyzing her problems. Yet she did not take a small but important step toward creating a revolution from within.

Sidestepping the Problem Pit

Let's apply the focus on wiring to medical problems. Instead of thinking what medicine you need, what device is right for you, or what procedure you should have next, check to see if it's really just a wiring issue. Taking sleeping pills does produce sleep, but it's not the same sleep that you get when you are dog tired from a day of hiking the hills, making passionate love, and bringing pies to the food bank.

The other day, I was doing a consult for Barbara who is 28, and she told me her story. She had been diagnosed with an eating disorder, panic attacks, anxiety, acid reflux, and insomnia. She listed off her diagnoses as if they were her identity, but really, the only thing wrong with her was that she was stressed. She had a few too many stress-inducing wires that needed to be weakened and broken. Yet her mind focused on her problems, so she was wiring herself to think of her life in terms of problems.

In EBT, you stop giving your power to the problems, and instead focus on how many moments of joy you experienced that day. How many times did you switch your brain to joy to break those errant wires that are messing with your life? And when you change your focus, those wires that ramp up problems change. You are weakening them. You are breaking them. One by one most stress symptoms fade. Medications, devices, and procedures? You begin to need fewer of them. You stop thinking of yourself in terms of problems. Instead, you think about the abundance of joy in your life!

What's a Circuit?

If your attention is turning to wiring, let's look at what a circuit is. A circuit is a string of neurons that carries the instructions of how you respond to a particular stressor. It is the chemical and electrical flow that determines whether you move through stresses or become stuck in them. There are three phases to these circuits.

The brain's emotional radar quickly appraises each new stimulus.

- The first phase of the circuit is quick emotional processing. In an instant, the brain compares the incoming information with the spate of wires from past experiences. If several are similar, it chooses the wire that is the most dominant, the strongest one. If there is no similar wire, the brain will lay down a new one.

- The second phase of the circuit is neocortical. The emotions from the emotional brain reach the thinking brain and mix with thoughts. In this phase, you figure out consciously how you feel and what you need.

- The third and final phase of a stress circuit is corrective action—an adjustment that alleviates stress and is rewarding.

This pattern is universal, that your response to life has an emotional phase followed by a neocortical phase, and last you find some corrective action that moves you back toward a favorable physiologic state. Yet there are two kinds of circuits—joy and stress—each of which creates a very different immediate experience and long-term consequences.

The Joy Circuit: Pristine and Perfect

The first kind of circuit is the joy circuit. The emotional response is in proportion to the stimulus at hand, not over- or under-reacting to stress. The emotion is balanced and travels up to the neocortical brain, which identifies the accurate feeling, finds a need that is reasonable, and leads to a corrective response, which returns you to the optimal state of joy. This is also called a homeostatic circuit. *Homeostasis* is the capacity to maintain stability by staying constant.

What's important about this circuit is that it minimizes unnecessary pain, nails what is really going on, and takes a corrective action that returns you to joy. Joy is the optimal state of physiology and that's the goal of the homeostatic circuit.

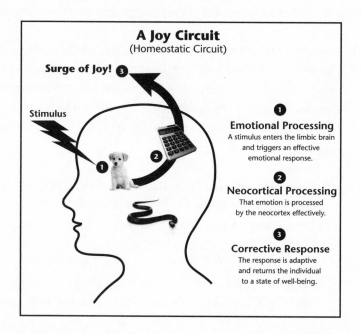

A Joy Circuit
(Homeostatic Circuit)

Surge of Joy! ❸

Stimulus

❶
Emotional Processing
A stimulus enters the limbic brain and triggers an effective emotional response.

❷
Neocortical Processing
That emotion is processed by the neocortex effectively.

❸
Corrective Response
The response is adaptive and returns the individual to a state of well-being.

The nature of homeostasis is to make the small adjustments necessary to keep that perfect balance, or as close as possible to it. Think of this circuit in terms of a thermostat set so the heat goes on if the room temperature is 65 degrees and the air conditioner starts up if the temperature reaches 80 degrees. Your guaranteed system will maintain a temperature within that narrow range, and that is just what the joy circuits do—they bring you back to balance within a narrow range. They pay attention, respond effectively, and end up in an adaptive, positive state. Mission accomplished.

This circuit is a *negative feedback loop,* which means that it self-corrects. Upon receiving information that your system has crossed one of its limits—sensing this negative information—your response sends the brain back toward the optimum direction of well-being. This feedback loop ushers you once again back to that comfortable range. This is protective, and has many benefits, but also has some drawbacks. The homeostatic wire is always self-correcting, so when you feel a surge of joy in your body, it will fade. You return to feeling balanced, not highly rewarded. That's how the circuit works—to get the highs requires consciously using the tools over and over again to create that joy. The buzzer does not get stuck on joy easily.

So in order to spend more moments of the day in joy and train the brain to become comfortable there, you can't go on autopilot. You must be constantly mindful, with focused effective practice over time switching the brain from stress to joy over and over again. In time it begins to stay in joy for longer, but given the nature of the circuit, triggering surges of joy is a lifelong practice.

The Stress Circuit: Diving into a Black Hole

The other kind of circuit—the stress circuit—is the problem. It is the triggering of this circuit that creates most of the unnecessary suffering in life. You know the feeling of being "triggered"—the state where you know you are overreacting, but if anyone tells you that you are, you would deny it as if your life depended on it.

The stress circuit triggers a prolonged and intense stress response that has no redeeming features other than the fact that it is better than nothing. The emotional response either blows the entire situation out of proportion, creating problems where there are none, or is shuts down and turns off emotions when there really is imminent danger. Most of the time, it overreacts.

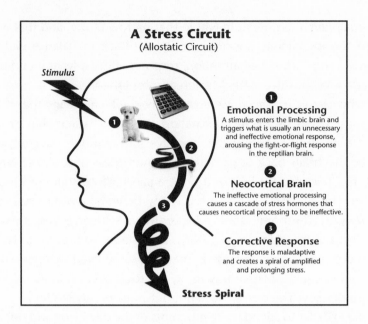

A Stress Circuit
(Allostatic Circuit)

Stimulus

1 Emotional Processing
A stimulus enters the limbic brain and triggers what is usually an unnecessary and ineffective emotional response, arousing the fight-or-flight response in the reptilian brain.

2 Neocortical Brain
The ineffective emotional processing causes a cascade of stress hormones that causes neocortical processing to be ineffective.

3 Corrective Response
The response is maladaptive and creates a spiral of amplified and prolonging stress.

Stress Spiral

The stress circuit isn't like the joy circuit—once that stress buzzer is turned on, it tends to stick. Someone cuts in front of you on the highway, and you're triggered, and you can't shake that rattled feeling. The weight of knowing the project is due next Friday and you haven't a clue how to start it grates on you. Rather than a feeling that flickers among relatively balanced states, when a stress circuit is aroused, it creates a bad mood that echoes through your emotional brain for a day, for a week, for what feels like a lifetime.

So what happened to trigger this stress circuit? During the emotional-processing phase, there is a glitch. The threat may be small, but the brain overestimates its intensity, making a mountain out of a molehill. And the brain triggers an unnecessary, irrational, fight-or-flight response. Off and running is a cascade of stress hormones, which soak into the neocortex, causing a serious problem. When the overblown emotional brain finally sends its emotions to the neocortex to process, they are way out of proportion with reality. And at this point, the neocortex is under the influence of the fight-or-flight stress hormones, so it has become rigid, unimaginative, repetitive, and ineffective. It even forgets what the original stress was, but remains confused and stressed out about being stressed out.

If you encountered the same stimulus but one of those pristine, homeostatic circuits was triggered, you could easily blow off the stress. It's just a momentary lapse into unnecessary stress, but we're talking an allostatic circuit here. It's extreme! *Allostasis* is defined as maintaining stability by changing. The status quo won't work; fine tinkering isn't enough. So the brain calls out all the troops and makes a systemic request for doing whatever it takes to return to a semblance of well-being.

And that all-out call to action is prolonged because this circuit is a *positive feedback loop,* which means that the fine tuning of homeostasis, with its clear limits—the equivalent of the heat going on at 65 degrees and the air conditioning going on at 80 degrees—is out the window. Instead, there is no thermostat, no heating and air conditioning, no limits. The stress response is triggered and there is no stopping the response. It is like a black hole in space, and once you step into it, who knows where you go?

Because the neocortex is hampered and can't figure out what corrective action will actually bring you back into balance, striving for stability becomes a constant game. Let's say a stress circuit is triggered by the disapproving glare of your boss. Your neocortex tries to process the emotion, but because it is under the influence of the chemical cascade of the fight-or-flight response, it decides on the corrective action of eating a cookie, rather than what you really need, which is to take a deep breath and get a reasonable view on the situation at hand. While eating the cookie does make you feel better in the short term, it triggers another kind of stress. This adds to the overall stress load, obscuring the clarity of the neocortex even further.

What happens to that adaptive, healthy, spot-on corrective action of the homeostatic circuit? It is not even under consideration, because this is a stress response and there are no shut-off valves available. So what can you do to turn it off? Emotions aren't under control. Thoughts are extreme. Attention is scattered or so rigid that you can't clear your mind.

What is left? You could always just wait it out and find that it dissipates in time, but that's not completely consistent with the pain of a full-blown stress response. It's really hard to tolerate. What's more, you forget what the original stress is, and when the stress buzzer is stuck on, you aren't even thinking about the original insult. Instead you are stressed about being stressed, and a mushroom of upset engulfs you. You feel lost, overwhelmed, and confused. So what do you do?

You draw upon the power of reward to swamp stress. You could be in a horrendous meeting with everyone arguing, and if a joy circuit had been triggered you could bring up a compassionate thought and swamp the stress. But unfortunately, no eudonic rewards are available now because the prefrontal cortex has been doused with cortisol. Focused attention? No. Spacious room for kindness during a fight-or-flight response? Forget it. All you have is the default reward, the hedonic pleasures, so this is where you turn. You use pleasures for pleasure's sake and to avoid stress. And these hedonic rewards will do, but not in moderation, because after all your brain is responding as if a hungry lion were nipping at your pants, and you have to do something extreme to counteract that extreme stress. You stomp out of the meeting. You throw a verbal dagger at your co-worker. You go to the vending machine and buy candy or take a walk to get a cigarette. You aren't in your joy.

Loving Your Circuits

Each of us has a bucket full of joy circuits and a bucket full of stress circuits. There are no bad circuits, just different consequences of firing them. Although stress circuits bring you closer to a semblance of balance, they do exact a price from you. All those cookies, the evenings lost to drink, the popped pills, and the endless array of excesses add to your wear and tear. For each trip into allostasis, each triggering of a stress circuit, there is a price to pay.

Yet I believe in loving all those circuits, even the stress circuits. They do serve a purpose. How else would you escape that hungry lion or the speeding car headed toward you? So how do you approach the stress circuits? With compassion—after all they were wired before the age of three, during times of stress and trauma, or by sheer repetition, typically of which you are not aware.

In a way, you'll love them, you'll not judge yourself for having or for triggering them, and you'll have a deep conviction that breaking those stress circuits will lead to something good. Healing the hurts leads to a depth of wisdom and maturity that people who have never had unthinkable pain do not know.

This is not about the joy circuits being "good" or stress circuits being "bad," even though the consequences of triggering these two are quite different. You have those stress circuits when you need them, and thank God for that, but you can also start using tools to break them, when you are ready and in good time.

SETTLING IN

The next time I saw George was two weeks later. That may have given him time to think about using the method and to see whether his initial enthusiasm lasted. What was important to me was that he started experimenting with the ideas of the method, and if he wanted to use it to set up a plan for getting support. The training is easier and more fun when done in community, with others who have the same goal: becoming wired for joy.

When George arrived, he looked as beleaguered as before.

"How may I help?" I asked.

"I don't know. This isn't a good time for me to do EBT. My daughter is seven months pregnant and can hardly move from the couch. She speaks to me with contempt or she doesn't talk at all. You should hear how she treats me!"

I sighed, nodded, and listened.

"I came today, but I can't do this. Emotions don't appeal to me. I need something tangible."

"Like a wire?"

"I don't get wires. I know I eat too much. I know I drink too much. That's something I can tackle."

"Maybe you should go on a diet or swear off alcohol. There are lots of programs that focus on that."

"I've done that."

I said nothing.

George said, "Why do again what hasn't worked before?"

"I'm here to support you, but this is a brain program. It helps to know your equipment."

"I can do that."

"Okay, then I want you to be able to differentiate a stress circuit from a joy circuit in your own life. Sketch out for me one of each kind that was triggered last week."

"It was a week out of hell. There were only stress circuits."

"That's impossible."

"I have every reason to be stressed."

"Stress is optional. There are no lions in your home."

"That's debatable."

"I want you to give a mental picture that is completely clear about one episode of a triggered stress circuit. I want you to outline the three phases of the circuit so that you know what is happening in your brain."

George reached into his pocket and pulled out a pack of cigarettes.

I was in shock. Was he considering lighting up in my office? Then my body relaxed, as I said, "I'm worried that you aren't aware that there is no smoking in this building."

"Do you really follow all the rules?"

"I can't stand the smell of cigarettes, and yes, I follow the rules."

"I stopped eating junk food, and I started to have this craving for a cigarette."

"That's why we don't overemphasize lifestyle at first. If it is not one stress symptom, then it's another. By the end of the session today, I want you to have identified a time in the last week when you were triggered . . ."

". . . with each circuit, right?"

"Yes, and come up with a plan for support. You are not an island."

George was now visibly irritated. I was happy to support him, but only if he would meet me halfway. Starting is not easy. Then there is a honeymoon when people think they are wired for joy. Finally, the deeper work begins where they clear away the circuits from the past that were wired early in life, make solid the circuits of a new, more effective way of processing daily life.

"It was Squeaky."

"Take me step by step through the circuit, starting with the stimulus and phase one, the emotional response."

"I was in the kitchen and Squeaky walked in and said, 'There is no decent food in this house.'"

"That was phase one of the circuit."

"Correct."

"That's the quick emotional processing phase."

"Instant rage," said George. "I felt this burn in my belly, worse than heartburn, followed by a stealthy knife in my chest."

"What happened in phase two?"

"I couldn't think. My eyes were popping out. Then before I could respond, he opened the fridge, took the last piece of chicken from the meat drawer, and grabbed two bananas from the bowl on the kitchen table. Then he marched out of the room."

"The third phase? What was your corrective action, what did you do to get back to balance?"

"I have no idea."

"That's normal. It's a stress response. Your mind goes blank or you start obsessing."

"I stayed in the kitchen, mindlessly reading the paper, and when Kate got home I unloaded on her. I was outraged that Ace's houseguest had the gall to be so demanding, so hostile, so . . . entitled!"

"So your response was ineffective?"

"I did what I always do. I fume. Then I complain. Then I blank out. Then I do nothing. I've been doing that since I was ten years old."

"That makes sense. Did you get back to feeling joy?"

George chucked. "No. Absolutely not. For three days I was stressed. I handled it pretty well. I popped antacids and stayed in my den."

"Great, you've got down what a stress circuit feels like. Now, let's track a joy circuit."

"Simple. I didn't have any."

"There's no rush. There is no question in my mind that you triggered some of those circuits. I can wait."

"Ace. We were watching television together, and I was wondering if she was going to start a fight, but then I looked over at her on the couch and I remembered her as a little girl. I felt love for her. I was grateful she was home, and I felt like telling her that."

"Did you tell her?"

"I'm not sure. Well, yes, I did. I reached over and patted her on the knee, and I smiled at her. She smiled back."

"Did you feel your surge of joy?"

"Actually, I did."

"Great. You're set. You know how both kinds of circuits work. Now you need some support."

"That's why I have you."

"I am your EBT coach."

"That's what I want. A coach."

"I see you for an hour a week. That's not going to be enough to create a revolution from within. You need connections, other people to practice the tools with."

"I have no interest in listening to other people's problems."

"I assumed that would be the case."

George said, "How did you know that?"

"Stress. It can make you want to roll up in a ball and conserve energy, to isolate."

"Of course I isolate. I'm in great company when I'm alone."

"A basic expectation of EBT is that you do connections to practice the tools. Each one takes 3 to 20 minutes, and you do at least three connections per week. The reason is that it speeds up your progress. When we added that element about 15 years ago, there were lots of benefits. The training was more fun. People were in community with people who had the same vision. And the rewiring speeded up. George, you don't have to be in a group if you don't want to. But you need to make connections."

George paused for a moment, deep in thought. Then his face brightened, and he said, "I can do that. I will connect with Kate, Ace, and Squeaky. Kate is in an EBT group, and maybe Squeaky and Ace will try it out."

"Great."

George smiled, and sat back in his chair. Perhaps he was going to do this work.

I asked, "Do you want to start using the tools with them?"

George rubbed his chin and said, "No, not yet."

"Then this week, start being more aware of your wiring, when you're triggering each kind of circuit, and see where they lead you."

"To brain states . . ."

"Precisely."

Chapter 4

What's a Brain State?

Wires trigger you, but what happens then? The brain reorganizes itself to respond to the level of stress that it encounters. Each area of the brain is more effective in processing a particular level of stress, so the brain determines which area should be dominant and in charge. Then it shifts energy to that part of the brain. That area then takes over for as long as the brain is in that state.

It is an elegant, spontaneous, and universal process. Wiring triggers brain states. Arouse a joy circuit, and you land in a brain state of relative balance. Arouse a stress circuit, and you land in a brain state of stress. The five brain states that have been identified are so diverse that it is almost as if you have five different people inside you. In each state, every aspect of your functioning is significantly different.

Who Is in Charge?

The more stressed you are, the more you trigger extremes of thoughts, emotions, and behavior. You are taught to focus on those specific extremes. The physician does a differential diagnosis to determine whether a patient is depressed or anxious, drinking too much, or overeating. That makes perfect sense if the plan is to prescribe a medication for mood or give advice for a bad habit. Yet that can easily take away your focus on the true problem: the wiring that leads to the brain state.

Getting accustomed to thinking in terms of brain states takes a while, but it has a lot of implications. To me, it is very reassuring to think that, despite all our differences, every last person on the planet is in one of the five brain states every moment of the day. Those stressed-out states? They are understandable. Everyone who is in a stressed brain state reacts in a fairly extreme way. Despite the variation in content, these patterns, which are the natural downstream effect of stress, have a lot in common: they work in the short term, tend to become repetitive, and become harmful in the long term. Your prefrontal cortex is being doused with stress chemicals that make your thinking extreme, rigid, and chaotic. In fact, you aren't in charge. The beast of the stress response is in charge, and you just come along for the bumpy and, at times, terrifying ride.

That's just one of your brain states. There are four others reflecting various levels of stress, but what is fascinating is that the more stressed people are, the more different from one another we are. The opposite of being in a stressed state is being in joy. In *Anna Karenina,* Tolstoy wrote: "Happy families are all alike; every unhappy family is unhappy in its own way." Families are like brain states. When people are peaceful and happy, they are remarkably the same. No matter who we are—rich or poor, male or female, black or white, gay or straight—when that flexible, resilient person is at the helm, we are bright, clever, positive, loving, curious, and full of joy.

To Know Them Is to Love Them

Last week, I was at JFK Airport in New York, returning from a trip to give a talk on the method and to celebrate my daughter's 30th birthday. It was early on a Friday morning, and the place was packed with travelers, some fleeing the city for a weekend getaway, and others tired from a hectic week, gathering up their laptops and bags to head home. The international crowd spoke many languages, and there were parents chasing after toddlers and old people being pushed in wheelchairs to make their flights.

All of them had wires flashing—either stress circuits or joy circuits—that landed them in one of the five brain states, and they were living out the natural consequences of whichever state they were in. I could see myself bouncing among the brain states: happy about the presentation I had given, really tired after a very late night celebrating my daughter's birthday, and feeling aches and pains in my body that signaled a flu coming on. I was living the natural rewards and drawbacks of each of the states I was in, and yet I managed to feel a sense of compassion for myself. Here I was, 60 years old, in a crowded airport, really tired yet sublimely happy. I could see myself, a bit disheveled and in a definitely stressed brain state, under the control of the region of my brain that wasn't doing a very good job of taking care of me.

Yet just seeing myself in one of those stressed brain states, with the area of my brain that was a bit reactive taking charge, I felt affection for myself. Who would want to force themselves to be joyful all the time? It would be its own tyranny, and who needs that? Can you imagine my being in the airport, noticing that I was stressed out and arguing with myself that I shouldn't be stressed, analyzing what was wrong with me and, in essence, getting in a fight with myself? Of course I would numb out, get depressed, feel ashamed, or make a hostile remark to the person who had the gall to be in my way.

Instead, I just settled down and connected to myself, allowing myself the freedom to move through all the states and to decide that in this lifetime, or at least for now, I'm not going to get into a fight with myself. I'm not going to reject myself, because then the enemy isn't the lion that is wandering into my camp, but it is within me.

Different Brain Areas at the Helm

Using brain states and the wiring that triggers them as our focus makes it all so much easier, because the shift among states is universal;

the higher the level of stress, the more primitive the brain area in charge. That natural shift in brain area is not necessarily convenient, but it is very effective. After the trip to New York, I would have liked to have felt vibrant and joyful, full of energy, and ready for more fun and games, but my body was tired. I had used up a lot of energy. My stress level was reflecting that, and the brain area in charge was not the lofty neocortex. I wasn't likely to come up with a great idea, or if I thought the idea was great at the time, by the next morning, after a refreshing night's sleep, it might sound rather lame. My survival need was to recharge, and my brain was taking care of that, shifting to my more primitive function, so that I was focused on not judging myself, minimizing the harm, and being aware that this state of stress would pass.

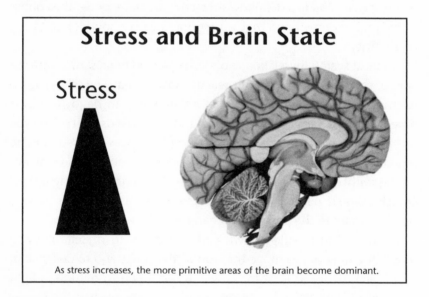

Stress and Brain State

Stress

As stress increases, the more primitive areas of the brain become dominant.

A Number for Each State

To make all this easier, let's assign each of the five brain states a number. Brain State 1 is joyous, while Brain State 5 represents a full-blown stress response, and the other states fall in between. That explains a lot because at each of the brain states, a different area of the brain is in charge, and which area of the brain is dominant has wide-ranging effects. When the brain stem—the reptile within—is in charge, you're going to be hostile. Have you seen how a snake strikes out? Or what about when that reptile shuts down and numbs out? Some extreme of mood will show up. What about when the warm connecting puppy of the limbic brain is in charge? Emotions start flowing, positive or negative. And when the neocortical brain is dominant, emotions are balanced, and you have the room to think magnificent thoughts and feel a warm sense of connection to others.

In Brain State 1, you're in the flow. Your whole brain is in balance; the circuits of all the areas are chattering quickly and easily; and you feel whole, balanced, and grateful to be alive. The neocortex, especially the prefrontal cortex, can think clearly, is attentive, and is attuned to the state of the emotional brain. Suppose a thought about an unpaid bill is aroused. The neocortex can handle that. It knows just how to process that stress back to a state of well-being. This is the brain state in which you can take control of your life, move with the flow of what is actually happening, and learn from your experiences. There are no problems, just inconveniences, just wires of stress to process back to your natural state of joy. You feel great.

In Brain State 2, you are slightly more stressed, but you feel balanced and generally good. It is the meat and potatoes state of being, in which you are aware of all the feelings, positive and negative. That is as it should be. Emotions are the sensitive motivators for you to take action, so the negative balanced feelings and the positive balanced feelings are equally helpful. The positive feelings are not good and the negative ones are not bad. Being aware that you feel some fear causes you to back up a little, before things become more dangerous. Noticing that you are angry gives you a chance to make a corrective action before you become hostile. The brain area in charge is a small slip away from neocortical, more influenced by the limbic brain.

In Brain State 3, you're a little stressed. Emotions are signaling that things are amiss, things need to be reckoned with. Some people notice that emotions are ramping up, particularly negative ones; others notice that emotions are beginning to shut down. Perhaps you are mired in thinking too much, to the exclusions of being emotionally aware. The limbic brain is now in charge.

In the last two states—4 and 5—you are clearly stressed, with the lower areas of the brain in charge. That stress shows up in two general ways, and that varies depending upon whether your brain tends toward shutting down emotions or ramping them up. Some people are hyperaroused and the feelings are overwhelming. Others tend to find their emotions oddly missing. Both are normal and part of the landscape of the reptilian brain taking over: extremes rule when you are stressed out!

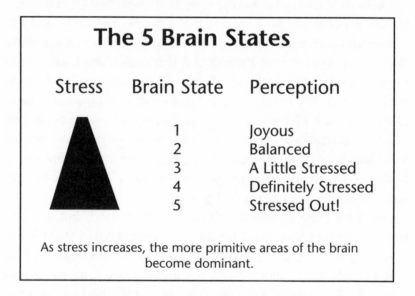

The 5 Brain States

Stress	Brain State	Perception
	1	Joyous
	2	Balanced
	3	A Little Stressed
	4	Definitely Stressed
	5	Stressed Out!

As stress increases, the more primitive areas of the brain
become dominant.

In the more stressed states—4 and 5—the prefrontal cortex is not very functional, and that has some repercussions. If you think about how you get safety in your life, what might come to mind is your home, your loved ones, or your job. Yet from a brain standpoint, what gives you safety is that you know what is going on emotionally, that your prefrontal cortex is conscious and is checking out what is happening in the emotional brain on a moment-to-moment basis. Any slight detachment from accurately reading the emotional brain has risks. Returning to the story of me in the airport, if I didn't know my number, how could I manage myself? If my prefrontal cortex were rigid, forgetful, and not attuned to the emotional messages, I'd forget to drink water, I would start obsessing about the writing project that was due and, in general, I would do a lousy job of managing myself. This would trigger more stress symptoms and land me in an even worse state of being. The focus on thinking rather than emotions is a major reason that so many highly intelligent, highly educated people have so many stress symptoms: they learned early in life to get their moment-to-moment security—safety, nurturance, love—from thinking and doing, rather than from their emotional connection to themselves.

The other source of safety is your reasonable expectations—a clear, flexible expectation that keeps you focused on moving toward some positive outcome. As you read this page, an expectation is holding you in the process. It might be, *I expect myself to do the best I can to read this so I understand how to feel my best*, or *I expect myself to do my best to understand this method and see whether I want to use it.* Yet imbedded in those expectations about your current situation are more profound and often unconscious expectations, such as that your life matters, you have power, or you can learn. These basic expectations are usually wired early in life. When stress mounts, your expectations are more likely to become unclear so you feel lost or unreasonable, directing you to neglect or even abuse yourself. That's what makes these stressed states that are triggered by allostatic circuits so frightening, because you have lost sight of your emotional state, and the expectations that hold you in some state of safety are either missing or counterproductive.

This is why getting to Brain State 1 is so important. Once you are there, it is easy to feel great, for you are aware of your emotional state and feel connected to yourself—the reenactment of the secure connection between parent and child. What's more, your expectations are clear and reasonable, so you feel secure that you are moving forward in the game of life. Things may not be perfect, but they will work out! Since most of your happiness is actually the "get up and go" of anticipating pleasure, you can feel great, even though your situation, to a casual observer, would seem miserable. In the brain states of stress, you lose that chemical safety net, so even if your situation is otherwise objectively great, you feel hopeless, lost, and in peril.

Other than Brain State 1, Brain State 4 is the most productive state, the blessed state, even though your emotions are churned up and your mood is extreme. You arrive at that state because a stress circuit has been triggered, and if a wire is triggered, it is open and fluid—ripe for change. The wires that are most problematic are usually encoded early in life and are thick, like ropes. When you are in Brain State 4, you can find that rope and begin to whittle away at it, weakening or even breaking it. If you are a little less stressed, say in Brain State 3, your capacity to identify that wire is compromised. On the other hand, when you are in Brain State 5, the lions are chasing you and your attention turns to survival. You are too confused and overwhelmed to focus on any one circuit, let alone have the neocortical control to use a tool to break it. That is why self-directed rewiring of your brain, using repeated experiences, is favored by being in moderate, but not excessive stress—that is, in Brain State 4.

Brain State 5 is amazing, because, on the one hand, it is really toxic. The reptilian brain is at the helm, and you find yourself in the vortex of the toxic spiral of stress. You feel lost and overwhelmed, which is why flipping on the television or texting a friend feels so good. You want to connect with something, anything, because your capacity to connect with yourself is severely compromised. That's the state in which there is not one stress symptom, but a whole party of them, and because the brain better remembers what happens in highly stressed states, whatever happens in this state can quickly become a circuit that is like thick, bristly rope. Yet when the clouds are darkest there is this lining of light, and that's how Brain State 5 is.

Mary Dallman, a pioneer in stress research, sees it that way—that in the darkest moment, if you really look for it, you'll notice a thin band of light. For under that state of 5, when you are desperate beyond belief, can be a shift to Brain State 4, when you can nab that offending circuit and break it. Sometimes, it can even turn into the brain state of 1: under the pain is the joy.

EACH STATE'S CHARACTERISTICS

So each number is associated with a particular brain area and that brain area predicts what you'll experience in each aspect of your life. If you find that all you want from EBT is to understand the concepts, then this is the area of the book you'll find the most fruitful. Even if you never use the skills, understanding the characteristics of each brain state can make a remarkable change in your life.

I was giving a talk to a group of managers, and I showed a slide of the chart below. A woman in her mid-20s approached me after that talk and said, "That one slide, the brain state characteristics. That's revolutionary. How can any of us judge others, when everyone is in each of those states at some point?"

Then another woman joined in, but her take on it was quite different. She said, "This gives me control. If I know what brain state I'm in, I can prevent a lot of damage. When I'm at 4, it's not reasonable to talk with my teenage daughter about her curfew on Saturday evening. In fact, when she is at 5 and I'm at 4, no wonder we get into horrible arguments. It's not us. It's our wiring that triggers these brain states."

The EBT Brain States

	Thoughts	Feelings	Relationships	Spirituality	Behavior
1 -	Abstract	Joyous	Intimate	Connected	Optimal
2 -	Concrete	Balanced	Companionable	Aware	Healthy
3 -	Rigid	Mixed	Social	Unaware	Moderate
4 -	Reactive	Unbalanced	Needy/Distant	Disconnected	Unhealthy
5 -	Irrational	Overwhelmed	Merged/Disengaged	Lost/Obsessed	Destructive

People use brain states in different ways, but it usually takes some experimenting with them to see what rings true for you. Also, some people find that one or two of these characteristics are particularly telling. They can figure out their brain state based on how they respond in relationships or what their behaviors are like. An attorney who recently joined an EBT group I facilitate said, "The only column I need is the relationship column. I know precisely what number I am by how I respond to other people. When I'm at 5, I can tell because I feel suffocated by other people. I want to run away as far as I can get. When I'm at 3, I can easily be social and talk about what was in the *Wall Street Journal* that day, or about how my stocks are doing, or about sports. When I feel the walls come down, and my wife and I are spooning, curled up in bed together, I know I'm at 1."

Karen, who teaches fourth grade, was highly emotional and was using EBT not only to combat the exhaustion of her long days in the classroom but also in pursuit of coming to terms with weight issues that had plagued her since she was nine years old. She found that her thinking tipped her off to identify her brain state number. Karen told me, "My emotions seem to be always raging inside me. I know I'm very sensitive; I always have been. Yet if I tune in to how I'm thinking, I instantly know my number. If my mind is working well and I'm imaginative, then I know I'm at Brain State 1. When I start running the same thought through my mind over and over again, that means I'm definitely at Brain State 3."

Right now, just getting an idea of what the characteristics are, and how they make sense given what area of the brain is in charge, is enough. Later, we'll talk about how to put this information to good use.

Part of becoming acquainted with these ideas is having fun with them, to take the concepts you are reading about and play with them. Be curious and wonder what your brain state is right now, and your child's brain state, and your co-worker's. Later in this book, when you read about the tools, the best way to approach them is to play with them, too. I remember listening to a physician who was coming to an introductory group on the method say, "I can't figure out the numbers, so I just try out the tools. When one of the tools works, then I know my number." That was the first time I had heard of a person using the method backward, but it works! Because the brain processes incoming stimuli so differently in each of the states, each tool only works to switch the brain back to joy for one state. This comes in handy, offering another way to figure out your number.

What follows is a snapshot of how each characteristic changes as the brain state changes. As you read, consider which of the areas could be the most telling for you, giving you the information that helps you figure out your state. If this all seems like more information than you want to hear, it works to return to the basics. When you are at 1, you feel great. When at 2, you feel good; at 3, a little stressed; at 4, definitely stressed; and at 5, super stressed out!

Thoughts: From Abstract to Irrational

Brain State 1: Abstract: Have you ever noticed that you get your best ideas when you're standing in the shower feeling the warm water beat down on your shoulders and the safe womb of the shower stall separating you from the cares of the day? Some people think best when shaving, when going for a run, when laughing with friends, or when daydreaming on an easy Saturday afternoon. In Brain State 1, you can think abstractly; that is, you can think about your thoughts, weave new dreams, resurrect the old, and be at your mental best. You don't forget where you left the keys, and you intuitively know not only what you need but also what the situation calls for. You are functioning well, cognitively.

Brain State 2: Concrete: In any state other than Brain State 1, the impact of the cascade of stress hormones takes its toll on the neocortex. In Brain State 2, your thinking is a bit more concrete. Gone is the magic of those fabulous ideas, finding just the right solution to the problem that nobody else even considered; however, you are still very functional. You think clearly and can go about your business of getting things done.

Brain State 3: Rigid: In Brain State 3, you lose your edge and now are rather rigid in your thinking, not quite "black and white" thinking, but definitely thinking in ways that are not flexible or imaginative. The neocortex, increasingly affected by stress hormones, narrows its focus and becomes set in its ways. You keep coming back to the same point even when you sense that nobody is really understanding what you are saying or finding your ideas terribly useful.

Brain State 4: Reactive: In Brain State 4, your thinking is clearly compromised. You get in ruts of thoughts, and part of that stubbornness means that you will not say you are wrong. You stick with some impossible idea as if your life depended upon it. Now the stress hormones add a tone of combativeness to your thinking. Whether your archenemy is within or without, you find yourself polarized. Cut loose from one extreme thought, you miss the middle ground, instead gravitating reflexively to the opposing extreme. The neocortex's natural fallback position during stress is trying to figure things out, analyzing problems, reworking the past, and obsessing about "what if's."

Brain State 5: Irrational: When the reptilian brain dominates, you can become rather irrational. You are so driven by the stress hormones that you grab onto an idea and force it through, no matter what. If a lion were chasing you, you can see the utility of rigid, narrow thinking. Yet it doesn't get you very far in the boardroom or the bedroom. In essence, stress has taken away your logical orderly thought, and now the neocortex begins making up stories, trying to find some safety in construing what could possibly be going on. The boss is out to get you. Your partner never really loved you. The whole world makes no sense. And the stress can make you completely forget what happened when you were in that state. Have an intense argument with a loved one, and the next day, you really don't remember what you said or did. It is not a convenient omission, but the truth. Stress has made you—at least for that moment—irrational!

Feelings: From Joyous to Overwhelmed

Brain State 1: Joyous: In Brain State 1, emotions aren't just positive, like the high you get from eating ice cream or slipping into a hot bath. The brain is so balanced that you feel a sense of peace, unity, and even sadness. Every intensive, joyous state is joined by sorrow. Even the strongest love is colored by intense longing, yet the bad feelings don't feel all that bad. You feel so *alive* that the valence of the emotion doesn't matter that much. You feel a swirl of intense wondrous emotions and are in love with your life, even the grittiness of it. Without that grittiness, positive emotions stay safely at Brain State 2, which is so ordinary, so devoid of spiritual magic, so separated from your capacity for boundless love. Instead of being detached from reality on a false high—like one you might get from partaking in a hedonic reward—you are grounded in your body, aware of your sensations and the expansiveness of life, and feeling as if in your own existence is a universe of meaning. It is the pleasure that you were born to have, and ultimately what motivates the survival of the species in the long term. It is the pleasure that chases away false attachments and addictive drives, for you are safe, you are loved, you are at one.

Brain State 2: Balanced: As stress increases, emotions become more extreme and tend toward the negative. In Brain State 2, you are aware of the positive and negative feelings, the information the neocortex requires to respond effectively to the moment, to figure out your needs, and do a reasonable job of meeting them. The emotions are balanced, so you feel happy and sad, not elated and depressed. Anger is red hot, but it stops short of hostility; guilt is not debilitating but a blessing, because it alerts you to your power and to what you can learn from past experiences.

Brain State 3: Mixed: In Brain State 3, feelings are yet more negative, but if you express the negative ones, the positive feelings will return, and they will feel genuine and soothing. You may begin to shut off your emotions as stress begins ramping up and notice that you are all in your head, thinking rather obsessively, analyzing everything. Or you may notice that feelings are more easily aroused. Instead of being present in the moment and aware of your emotions, you tend to distance from them a bit or busy yourself by manufacturing them. In all, you feel a little stressed but nothing out of the ordinary for negotiating the various demands of the day. You remain rather functional and move through your day relatively well when in Brain State 3.

Brain State 4: Unbalanced: In Brain State 4, emotions take a significant turn toward states of imbalance. Instead of feeling angry, you're hostile; rather than sad, you're depressed and powerless. The balanced feeling of fear turns into chronic anxiety or panic, and the guilt, which in more balanced states leads you to identifying what you could do differently, turns into shame or self-persecution. You don't just evaluate your behaviors; you judge and condemn yourself. Some people find that they gravitate to false highs rather than these unnecessary lows. They become so elated that they forget to pay the light bill or so manic that they burn themselves out. On a false high, fantasy can rule, as you live in another world, an altered state, and all the crucial aspects of life go unattended. Another possibility is shutting down feelings even more than in less stressed states, and feeling just fine in a way, except that you wonder where your feelings went. Other people have feelings, but yours are oddly missing. In this state, you tend to attribute your unbalanced emotions to the situation at hand. It's that lousy boss, the difficult teenager, or the maxed out credit cards that make you feel so bad, rather than the wiring that is triggering that state and the pile up of emotional residue from the past that is amplifying the difficulties of your current situation.

Brain State 5: Overwhelmed: In Brain State 5, strange things occur on the emotional front. In a way, this state can feel like an odd variation of Brain State 1. Aeron Hicks, a long-time minister of the method often says, "The brain states are a circle, not a line, with Brain State 5 and Brain State 1 sitting side-by-side." The terror you feel in Brain State 5 is a hair's breadth away from the glorious state of 1. If you get close enough to the gritty dark side of life, the light side sweeps you off your feet and shows you the way to nirvana. Yet in Brain State 5, emotions can be so extreme and negative that you are sure you've crossed the line one too many times and will never recover, never return to any state of safety and repose. That disorienting terror often appears as confusion, a feeling of being overwhelmed, outright hostility, or toxic shame. In fact, it can be so extreme that it burns out and returns you to Brain State 1 if you have a sharp eye and look for it, or more often, especially if you aren't looking for Brain State 1, to Brain State 4, where you feel unbalanced—way high, way low, or numb.

Relationships: From Intimate to Merged or Disengaged

Brain State 1: Intimate: Only in Brain State 1 are you truly intimate with another. Intimacy is the experience of being separate from another but close. The comfort of the mirroring of two limbic brains, resonating in connection, is the greatest joy on earth. The misconnection or disconnection between two souls spreads toxic levels of stress hormones in an instant, and one rejecting glance from the object of one's desire can bring you to your knees. Emotional connection is a primary need. Monkeys go without food in favor of the warmth of nurturing, and lovers know how when the heart soars everything else seems somehow unimportant. Moments of soul-touching intimacy seem mystical, and perhaps you are in such a state of balance that you are not only in secure, loving connection with each other but also with the spiritual—something greater than yourself. You have spacious feelings of love that radiate outward and touch another, and you feel capable of loving all living beings. Love is so essential to human survival that it is gifted with surges of oxytocin that reward and soothe.

You can experience that closeness when you're at Brain State 1, because it is safe to do so. You are not diverting energy to self-preservation, as you would if stress were to mount. You can just be and allow others to just be. You can see the whole of yourself and others—the light side, the dark side, and all. The circuits of connection are aroused at once and although it feels like a loving connection to another, the depth of connection you feel is to yourself—the aliveness, the peace, and spiritual love create a crescendo of pleasure. In Brain State 1, it feels safe and even nurturing to have tissue-paper-thin boundaries with another, for you know you won't lose yourself or surrender, because your connection to yourself is intact and sturdy. That intimacy with yourself assures that should something change and you needed, in an instant, to have a vault-thick boundary, you could do that. What's more, if you were rejected, it would hurt, but you would not reject yourself. You could still come home to that secure awareness of yourself.

Brain State 2: Companionable: When you are balanced but your state stops short of conferring the capacity to see into the hearts of others, compassionate yet secure relationships shift. Rather than intimate, they are companionable. That spark of love morphs into the steady awareness of another, the sharing and laughter and play, but your very essence stands aside, slightly more protected. Relationships are enjoyable and rewarding, but the profound healing and delight of soul-touching love is outside your experience in Brain State 2. Affection abounds and the good times roll, and this is a functional connection that fills up your days, and, in general, feels good.

Brain State 3: Social: As stress increases, you begin compromising your connection to yourself. You're aware of your feelings, but you aren't sure which one is most important, and your thoughts are a bit rigid. So where does that leave relationships? They are social. You can shoot off e-mails, chat on the phone, connect with others on a superficial level much like toddlers play. They watch each other and play side-by-side, and that can be satisfying, particularly if you are four years old. Yet more and more, with stresses mounting, people give in and settle for social relationships, being glad that they at least have that connection. It is far preferable to watching television alone at home or working at the computer for an ungodly number of hours each day. In this state, you can easily engage in pseudo intimacy, for example sharing vital information with a stranger over the Internet, because the risks of adult intimacy—surrender or rejection—do not surface. Your disclosure amounts to an emotional freebee. There is nothing wrong with social relationships, but your soul hungers for that multi-layered experience of intimacy and the mirroring of that attachment. The emotional brain yearns to recreate the feeling of being seen—really seen—by a loving other. And you want to be really heard, not just the words but the nuances of the words; you want another to know your very essence. The same circuits that are downloaded into your brain from that early connection that processes stress cements the definition of connection. So you unconsciously repeat the early merging and distancing, the chaos and rigidity, even if it does not work, because the emotional brain prefers familiar bedfellows to surprises.

Brain State 4: Needy or Distant: Whereas the more mundane varieties of connection still hold rewards of an adaptive sort, as stress mounts, intimacy takes a sad turn. In Brain State 4, you are definitely stressed, your connection to yourself slips significantly, and the foundation of connection becomes shaky. The two fundamental drives fueled by stress—to merge or distance—worm their way into your encounters with others, and quite frankly, you use or lose people. There are no lions in the bedroom, but it sure feels like it when your brain is in this state. And if you don't know about brain states and that they pass, then you might think of yourself or your partner as pretty pathetic when it comes to love. Yet it is not you; it's just the universal impact of stress. People merge and distance as the drive to survive overtakes the capacity to love unconditionally, without strings attached, and without justification. Nobody says in their marriage vows, "I will give you unconditional love when I am in Brain State 1, but when I'm in stressed states, I'll naturally take an emotional hike or overwhelm you with my neediness." Yet these universal tendencies do crop up when cortisol has its way with you.

In EBT, we think of intimacy as occurring when you are aware of both your own feelings and needs and the feelings and needs of others. The emotional pipeline between two people is open and there is a giving and receiving of love. When stress mounts, the emotions start roaring and the prefrontal cortex is not very functional, so you lose connection with yourself. That's frightening, because connection is your safety valve and it's shutting off. You often lose sight of your own feelings and needs and fixate on the feelings and needs of others. You merge. Or you are so frightened by your loss of connection with yourself that you funnel every last shred of consciousness to trying to find it again. You distance, going into yourself, searching. Neither works, but hey, you're under the influence of a stress circuit, so that's how it is.

If you merge, you are trying to find safety. You can't find safety inside yourself, so you are hell-bent on getting that safety from the emotional state of another. You'll do whatever it takes—people pleasing, rescuing, manipulating—because unconsciously it feels as if your life is on the line.

If you distance, you are trying to find your own safety, and these pesky people keep knocking on the door, invading your cave, and generally getting in the way of your survival pursuit of that lost connection with yourself. Get in the way of a rampaging lion, and you can lose your life. Get in the way of a distancer's need to self-soothe and become the recipient of that ire—lashing out at you in whatever way he or she can: verbal assaults; hiding through overworking; or plugging into the television, food, alcohol, video games, or anything that gives a safe refuge. At Brain State 4, you feel under attack and need to find a safe haven for yourself.

At Brain State 1, unencumbered by the survival drives to merge and distance, you are genuinely loving. It is not you. It's your wiring.

Brain State 5: Merged or Disengaged: The drives to merge and distance in Brain State 4 only become more pronounced when you're under siege from a full-blown stress response. The nature of a stress response is that it can't last all that long, or it would kill you. Stress pioneer Bruce McEwen often refers to the plight of salmon, whose enormous burst of energy to swim upstream, which is fueled by cortisol, culminates in sufficient enough damage to cause their death. So the exhausting surge of stress hormones in Brain State 5, in time settles back into another state, perhaps Brain State 4 or 3, or even Brain State 1—as evidenced by the famous post-fight passion and amour. However, in the throes of fight or flight, thoughts, emotions, and behaviors are their most extreme, so who knows what can happen? And when it does, you either fixate on it or can't remember it ever happened. This is when allostatic circuits wired during early disconnection or trauma fire up and amplify your stress, so you feel tortured, abandoned, or lost. You're prone to use various exit strategies—drinking the whole bottle of wine, popping too many pills, or eating yourself silly. Your misguided attempt to fill the void only exacerbates the disconnection from self and others. Yet these moments in Brain State 5 live inside the unconscious memory systems of the emotional brain. Given enough ugly scenes at Brain State 5, you may wonder if you are a really toxic person who perhaps isn't suited for life on this planet. Yet, in truth, it is just a brain state, one that every person on earth is capable of experiencing; and although you are responsible for your actions and pay the price for your experiences in that state, it is just a state, triggered by a wire made up of neurons that cling to one another in particular patterns and wreak havoc in your life.

Spirituality: From Connected to Lost or Obsessed

Brain State 1: Connected: In much the same pattern as intimacy, your relationship with the spiritual changes in concert with the state of your brain. When you are in Brain State 1, you feel a rolling kind of connection to yourself, to others, and to the spiritual—however you define it: the spiritual forces on the planet; the awesome beauty of nature; the unity of humankind; a devotion to the evolution of the planet; a personal connection with God. You can touch the spiritual during a quiet moment of prayer, singing your lungs out, holding a newborn baby, or regarding the full moon. Although being in spiritual connection can be triggered by a thought, a sensation, or an action, it is quintessentially emotional. For some who find Brain State 1 to be their resting place, spiritual connection can be amazingly enduring, the background music of their day, sometimes playing softly and other times loudly. More often than not it is fleeting, as you live at Brain State 2 and experience spikes of elevated emotions. Brain State 1 can be the ultimate sign of the brain state of joy, and when you experience that power, so profound and universal, it seems that every other power is dwarfed by comparison.

Brain State 2: Aware: In Brain State 2, you are somewhat aware of the spiritual. That background music plays in subtle strains, but still confers a sense of safety, if not supreme connection. You know what you should do to be good people, and you have the balance to do those things more of the time, and now and then an appreciation for the greater meanings of life occurs to you as you inch toward Brain State 1. You consciously go out of your way for others, and take care of your responsibilities, knowing that there is a meaning to it all and you are your cooperative best in being part of the overall plan.

Brain State 3: Unaware: As stress mounts, and disconnection from self with it, the spiritual is not your top priority. Your purpose in life is not to follow your spiritual path; it's to get the job done, figure things out, and make it through the day in reasonable style, and with a measure of productivity. Emotions quiet down and thoughts are rigid, so you aren't expansive and considering the deeper meanings of your every act. Frankly, you're a little scattered, and the meaning of it all takes a backseat to the pragmatic matters of the day. You're a little stressed, and in that state the brain quickly sheds spiritual encumbrances in favor of the more pressing demands.

Brain State 4: Disconnected: As a sense of being threatened creeps up on you, emotions are unbalanced, and even more important, your expectations become unreasonable—too harsh or too easy—or unclear. Regardless, your sense of being safe quickly erodes because you have no clear, flexible—conscious or unconscious—expectations to enable you to hold onto yourself and envision a reward of meaning. Instead you default to a survival mode, in which you want what you want when you want it. If you didn't appreciate that this is just a brain state, you'd be horrified, because your every act, even those that look virtuous, are actually to serve one master: the ego. You are vulnerable to the stinginess of this brain state, and can one minute be in Brain State 1, doing things for all the right reasons, then the next minute slide right into Brain State 4, where your purposes shift, and you are doing that same kind act not out of kindness but out of selfishness. But this shift is natural. Part of being wired at 1 is lovingly accepting your tendencies to volley among all the brain states—even the gritty, ugly stressed states—and why unconditional love of self and others, and an endless capacity to forgive and begin again, is core to being your best self.

Brain State 5: Lost or Obsessed: When I think of the moments I spend in Brain State 5, feeling spiritually lost, I don't know whether to laugh or cry. Both seem in order, and after the emotions pass, a sense of acceptance follows. The emotional brain, in a full-blown stress response, grabs onto thoughts in obsessive ways so that you use religion in unspiritual ways or you simply feel so lost, so abandoned, and so angry at the universe, at God, and everything and everyone, that you are in terror. You are not only vulnerable to believing that all is lost, but to losing yourself into various false connections that appeal to your lost sense of goodness. To the extent that Brain State 1 feels heaven-sent, when you are in that caldron of stress of Brain State 5, you are in hell; nothing looks good to you, nothing at all, because you are so lost, so terrified, and so bone-chillingly alone.

Behavior: From Optimal to Destructive

Brain State 1: Optimal: In Brain State 1, stress appetites fade and the reward circuitry is so flush with feel-good neurotransmitters that it is easy and natural to live in the healthiest of ways. You simply don't care about sugary, fatty foods, and other various chemical pleasures seem superfluous. In a study of 100 people using the tools intensively for three days, 92 percent said that the drive to overeat had diminished. In that state of well-being, the chemicals that prop up your mood in stressed states are in ample supply. The rewards are flowing, and even the thought of how great you feel—your personal hold on vibrancy and zest—is enough to push away from the table, put on those walking shoes, and go for a hike. The rewards of intimacy are sending ripples of pleasure through your body, so you have an elegant sufficiency in life. You have no wants, your needs are met, and it is all so easy and good—and healthy.

Brain State 2: Healthy: At Brain State 2, your tendency is to behave in ways that promote the maintenance of your health. You remember to take the vitamins, stop off at the farmer's market for fresh produce, and walk the dog after dinner, and even feel like turning up the music and soaking in the natural pleasure of it all. Life is good, and you methodically go about the business of living in a healthy way most of the time. The brain strives to be in 1, and the difference between these two states shows up in small but important ways. Someone at work passes around a box of candy. Who needs candy when you are in Brain State 1? Nobody, because the chemical effects of that state are so deeply satisfying, and besides candy sticks to your teeth and carrying around a few extra pounds slows you down when you are running down the basketball court. But in Brain State 2, oh well, what's a little candy?

Brain State 3: Moderate: As stress mounts, you're a little frazzled and tend toward thinking too much and losing awareness of your emotions. You have things to do and problems to solve and that slight bit of detachment from your emotions translates into being less sensitive to your body's needs. Who cares if the sandwich has globs of mayonnaise on it, or if the salad comes drenched in Thousand Island dressing? You cut short your workouts or start depending upon them for mood management, because stress is piling up, and processing it internally isn't a priority. So your behaviors are moderate, not horrible, but instead of promoting your vitality, they begin to detract from it.

Brain State 4: Unhealthy: As stress increases, emotions become unbalanced and expectations unreasonable. You try to steady yourself and manage your mood through various behaviors, none of which involve reaching for a celery stick. What's most interesting to me about this brain state is that behaviors are extreme. In health care, we tick off the various bad habits, asking whether you smoke, drink too much, or eat too much; but it is not just one behavior that is unhealthy, it is nearly all of them, even in subtle ways. Many are socially acceptable, such as holing away at the gym while the kids watch television at home, or working so much that intimacy suffers. Either you can't get a good night's sleep or all you want to do is sleep. Come Saturday afternoon, you're on the couch curled up in blankets and sleeping the day away. Often, we think in terms of one or two bad habits, but the chemical cascade of stress hormones, and the imbalance of neurotransmitters, translates into a whole spate of behaviors that promote early aging and increase risk of disease.

Brain State 5: Destructive: The natural cravings and drives of Brain State 5 demand pleasure, so many people think they are in Brain State 1 when they are eating sugary, fatty foods or going on a drinking binge, but they're in a false 1, which is Brain State 5.

In Brain State 5, you don't think about tomorrow, because the time warp that tells you it will always be this way also blinds you to awareness of the consequences of your behavior. Your prefrontal cortex isn't in any shape to bring up thoughts of the virtuous meaning of what you are doing, so the access to surges of pleasure that motivate you, as well as quash the stress circuits and damp down your pain, aren't available. You're in terror, and relationships don't help much because you are merging and distancing, and the spiritual is no place to be found—in fact, you feel it has ditched you—so you have virtually no impulse control and compulsive drives ramp up. You do the logical thing: you try to meet your needs in whatever way you can because otherwise you face what feels like certain death—or at least something like that, such as being suffocated, beaten, or shamed.

It's a brain state that, when you come out of it, leaves you wondering where you've been. You may even forget how bad you felt once you're in another state. Which is why you then stand aside and judge yourself up one side and down the other for what you did that was not responsible, healthy, or socially acceptable. That judgment is part of the problem, because the soul so reviles shame and judgment that this has the opposite effect and makes you want to engage in that behavior more—with more vehemence, more gusto, and more desire. In addition, when you are in Brain State 5, you suffer from the other characteristics, including emotional imbalances (like false highs, unnecessary lows, and numbness) and cognitive difficulties (such as blanking out, not remembering, or obsessive thoughts). Add to that the misconnections with others and the spiritual, and who wouldn't go for a binge on whatever will alleviate the pain and bring some semblance of safety and reward—again and again and again?

A SWIRL OF STRESS SYMPTOMS

Most of us list our problems, one by one. But in EBT, we think in terms of systems and spirals of symptoms, which each affect the other. We recognize that if you treat only the behavioral stress symptom, for example, overeating, but not the other symptoms that keep it company in that state of stress, the treatment doesn't work so well. The silent partners of that state of stress are rigid thinking—the kind of thinking that keeps you going back to the same diet year after year, even though you always gain the weight back. It's the depressed or anxious mood that uses food to ameliorate or the gut feeling of being sorely alone and spiritually left out, which is worsened by relationships that are not intimate. All of it fits together, and trying to change one aspect without changing the others is woefully difficult and almost always ineffective. In fact, I don't recommend listing the whole all of stress symptoms, and then trying to wipe them out one by one. There are just too many!

So any momentary brain state is not the focus of intervention. If we spend most of our time in the homeostatic states, the brain states tend to flicker, but in the allostatic states? They easily and often become persistent, so your goal is to get unstuck from that stressed state by giving the brain repeated experiences in states of high-level well-being. You aim to establish a new set point, a new emotional comfort zone that is so much better that, on an unconscious level, you know there is no going back. You are finally home.

A REALITY CHECK

George came in for the next coaching session, and it was time for him to start moving forward with the tools. Most people start off right away with using the tools, but George needed to move a bit more slowly.

When he arrived, he looked discouraged. Perhaps the challenge of doing brain rewiring was getting to him, or things were not going well at home, with Kate and her shopping, Ace and her pregnancy, and Squeaky eating up his food.

"What did you accomplish this week, George?" I asked.

He looked at me with a glare, "Nothing." His face looked basset-hound sad.

I replied. "Yes you did. You came back!"

"I would have canceled, except you would have charged me, because of late notice."

I nodded. He didn't have the tools down yet, so we couldn't use this stress as moment of opportunity, a time to use the tools to find one of those errant circuits and break it.

"I'm happy you came back."

He sighed and said, "Nobody would connect with me."

"Not Kate, Ace, or Squeaky?"

"Turns out, his name isn't Squeaky, thank god. That's just what Ace calls him. His name is Ronald, and in addition to being a biking enthusiast, he's an attorney. He was interning with a law firm that always hires their interns, but the legal business is in a downturn. "

"Just like the drug companies?"

"Yes. So he is only out of work for a while, and I think he is interviewing with a firm today. But I've grown accustomed to him these days."

"He's not complaining about the food?"

George coughed a little, "No, but I didn't ask him to do a connection and use the tools with me. I started to ask Ace, but then I decided that it would never work. And I won't even ask Kate because she'll start using it to control me. She's already started asking me to check my number, in a critical way, as if I were a four-year-old."

"I feel sad hearing that."

He shook his head. "It's an awful way to live."

George's eyes looked sad. I said, "What did you figure out about brain states this week?"

"I think I'm wired at about a 2."

I laughed, "You're way ahead of me. I was talking about your brain state in the moment, not how it generally is."

He was undeterred. "I think I'm wired at 2."

"Okay, how did you figure that out?"

"Well, I'm pretty balanced. I don't have a lot of feelings, and these days I'm pretty easy-going."

I thought of what Kate had said about her husband, which was a slightly different picture. The point is to become comfortable with thinking in terms of brain states, so I followed whatever interested him, which seemed to be figuring out a person's emotional set point.

"Take Kate for instance. She's definitely at 5. She lives at 5. She never stops. I would call her hyperactive, because she is up in the morning by 5:30. Then she is compulsively cleaning the house. There is not one drawer in the kitchen that doesn't have everything lined up—the spices are in alphabetical order, the 50 kinds of plastic bags are organized by size, and the space in the refrigerator is totally assigned—there is one specific place for the capers, the hot mustard, and the soy milk. And if I dare to put something back in the wrong place, she fumes. It doesn't make sense because the basement, my area, has become a stockpile for shopping bags, and antiques, and it's a complete disaster. She has to have everything organized upstairs or she's a wreck, but in the basement, it's her personal stockpile, and she could care less whether it bothers me or not. She always gets her way, just like Ace."

Playing with Brain States

"Do you have your iPhone with you?"

He nodded.

"Just take it out, and let's figure out her number."

With that, George pulled his phone out of his pocket and opened up the application.

"Okay, think of the last 24 hours. Her thinking?"

"Concrete, functional, but not creative and abstract. I would say she is at 2."

"Feelings?"

"Actually, she is happy that Ace is home. I would say balanced. She used to be all over the map, but most of the time these days she is at 2."

"Relationships?"

"I don't know where to start on that one. With Ace, she is intimate. With Ronald she is intimate. Then there's me. She can't stand me. She has a huge wall up, either that or she is micromanaging me. Who is she to give me advice? I am not her project to fix. What kind of a woman would want to fix her husband? If she would just do it my way, clean up the mess in the basement, and loosen up a little bit, everything would be fine."

"What number is she in her relationship with you?"

George took another deep breath, and then said, "She is at 4."

"So we have a 2, a 2, and a 4."

George was still passionate about figuring out Kate's brain state when connecting with him. "No, my wife's full out disengaged from me," he amended.

"Okay, a 5 then.

"Spiritually, she is . . . I'm not sure."

"Aware, unaware, disconnected?"

"I think she's aware; that puts her at 2."

"Her behavior?"

"Well, she is changing. A month ago I would have said she was at 4. In the last week or so, I haven't seen her bring home as many shopping bags. She's been having coffee with Ace and Ronald in the morning. She's more relaxed, not running off to the gym as much. I would say she is a 2 or 3 in behavior."

With that, George touched the screen of his phone. Now all the information was entered in and he waited to see what her state was.

"Okay," he said. "That's about right. She's a 2. She's wired at 2, just like me."

Then he smiled. He had figured it out.

"George, what number are you now?" I asked.

"I don't know," he said.

As Others See Us

"It takes time to figure this all out. Sometimes it helps to take one characteristic at time, and see yourself as other people might."

George shrugged, "Okay, I can do that."

Then he touched the screen of his phone to clear away his recounting of Kate's numbers. Ultimately, George would figure out brain states without the application, but he was having a good time and so was I.

"Let's rate your thinking. If someone else was watching you carefully, what would he or she say?"

"My concentration is off, and I get in these ruts where I can't turn my mind off. That's why it so hard to sleep. My mind keeps thinking and thinking. That's definitely reactive, I would say, a 4."

"Great. What about your emotions?"

George sighed. "I'm still living in my den most of the time. I have not even had one interview, much less a job offer. Most of the time

I am numb. Then every once in a while, I lose it and slam a door or throw my keys. I would say a 4."

"Relationships?

"Well I couldn't get connections, could I? I think I'm getting an F at intimacy. That would be a 5."

"Are you sure? What about those tender moments with Ace, and you spoke so kindly about Ronald just now."

"Well, that's true. Then I'll give myself at 4." He touched the screen again.

Then he furrowed his brow and said, "Spirituality. I'm going to skip that one."

"That's fine."

He said, "I'm not a religious person."

Making a distinction between spirituality and religion was very important, because they aren't always in perfect synchrony.

"George, this is a brain-based method. It's not about religion. When the brain is in balance, and the reward centers are full of surges of neurotransmitters, many people feel connected to something that is bigger than themselves, however they define that. They are aware of the grace and mystery of life."

His eyes misted slightly, "It's been a long time since I've felt like that. In fact, I don't know if I have ever felt that way."

"Some people feel that unity when they are in nature."

"I went on a small plane with Marvin Dodd about ten years ago, and we flew to a rustic cabin in Canada. The river was right outside, and it was ice cold and roaring. The sky was bright blue. I really relaxed on that trip, and I was in awe of nature, being with my friend, and being outside fishing all day."

George held onto that vision of the cold, clean waters and the bright, blue skies, and I could see a sparkle in his eye.

Then he sighed and said, "I'd say I'm at 4, disconnected from the spiritual." Then he was done. He had answered all the questions, and he touched and screen and waited. "It says I'm at 4."

His ears turned red, and my mirror neurons caught wind of his rage. I felt a tightness in my chest. He said, "I don't want to be at 4.

I hate being at 4. I hate it that I have worked this hard in my life and I'm settling for being at 4. It isn't fair." Sadness came across his face, "I feel sad that my life is limited. I feel afraid that this is as good as it will ever get."

I noticed myself letting out a huge sigh, feeling his sadness, but not his fear, and hoping that he would catch the vision of him being at 1.

"It's all my fault. I was so separated from reality. I worked myself to the bone for that company, and now I'm paying the price."

"George, wasn't it reasonable to expect that you would?"

A bolt of light crossed his face. Instantly, he looked ten years younger. I knew he was at 1. The muscles in the face always show the brain state, and his joy was catching. I was feeling that liquid warmth in my chest, the sign of the reward centers surging.

"You're right. I was raised to work myself to death, that's what my dad did. I expected that if I was just a really good boy and did whatever the corporation told me to do, brought home the bacon, and made money for my family, that I would be safe."

"George, that's a circuit, that's a stress wire. You just nabbed it."

His eyes brightened, and he sat up straight in his chair.

"I did?"

"You must have been at Brain State 4, because you just used an informal version of the tool for that state, the one that nabs the circuits. You're on a roll; don't stop now. What is your unreasonable expectation—that circuit—that has been rattling around inside you since you were a kid?"

"I don't know. Maybe that I get my safety from doing what I am told."

"What is a more reasonable expectation? This is where you start breaking that circuit." I prompted him, "It's a reasonable expectation that I get my safety from . . ."

"I don't know where I get my safety from. Especially now."

"Look at those brain states, George. Which one is safe?"

"I don't think any of them is safe. I think I get my safety from knowing my number. At least then I can make a plan."

"Where is your number? Where does it come from?"

"It comes from inside. That's it. I get my safety from inside me."

I nodded and smiled. George had inadvertently used the tool for Brain State 4, and popped to Brain State 1. What an amazing man. He had stayed with it and switched his brain to a state of joy. He could well be on his way.

Chapter 5

How Brain States Get Stuck

The brain is an organ of habit. Feed it enough moments of stress, and it learns that stress is normal. The brain likes sameness, so anything novel is a threat. It's no wonder why it's so easy for the brain to become fixed in stress and see moments of joy as a threat. In a way, that works in your favor. Because the emotional brain is a follower, if you are mindful of your state and switch it to a favorable state over and over again, the brain can learn to establish a groove in the state of well-being.

Why doesn't that just happen naturally? Why aren't more of us wired for joy? The deck is stacked in favor of stress, partially because the brain is naturally anxious. Our ancestors who survived long enough to procreate and influence the gene pool were the anxious, vigilant ones, not the relaxed happy campers who failed to notice the rustling in the bush of that hungry lion. But there are other factors that come into play, too, for becoming stuck in stress is a process that begins early in life.

THE TENACITY OF EARLY WIRING

The earliest connection between parent and child begins to download the most fundamental processing of daily life—the intimate and essential wiring—into the emotional brain of the child. Nobody needs perfect parenting, but small yet important misconnections in the attachment between parent and child can lead to misconnections in the child's self-regulation that can last a lifetime. If you are wired to process stress ineffectively, you tend to manufacture stress. You're unaware of your emotions, misread them, or have no idea how to return to balance in an adaptive way.

What's more, the way you are wired early in life to process stress feels comfortable to you. It is stored in your unconscious memory systems, so you aren't even aware of what's happening. You just do it. Without even realizing it, you fan the flames of stress, encoding and strengthening stress circuits to a point where stress becomes the norm, the brain's set point.

Kate's early life was a perfect example. If we look in on Kate being raised, it all looks uneventful. Kate's mom, Marion, was an overthinker. She had never learned to honor her feelings and was chronically anxious, wired at Brain State 4. She loved Kate, but her thinking was reactive, her emotions somewhat negative, and her connection with Kate slightly off. It was hard for her to attune to Kate's feelings when she was so often overpowered by her own or lost in her thoughts. Her focus was on controlling the environment to make a stable home. Kate's father, Ralph, worked as an oil distributor six days a week just to make ends meet, but she saw him on Sunday morning when the whole family went to church. And in the evening they had a family dinner of baked potatoes, roast beef or chicken, iceberg lettuce salad, and a bowl of fresh fruit cut into small cubes. Dessert was ice cream— chocolate, vanilla, or mint chip.

Early in life, Marion's repeated contact with her infant downloaded into Kate's rapidly developing, and therefore highly plastic emotional brain, her own basic expectations about life, which in this case were that she had no power, that she didn't measure up, and that life was to be endured. With each contact, that wordless transmission of the circuits of basic expectation were transmitted by her facial expressions, words, and actions.

What's more, sometimes Marion was off the mark in reading Kate's emotional state, so the compass Kate needed to read her own was a little off, too. That internalization of the good parent—that sanctuary within—didn't quite form as well as it might have. And because Marion didn't know how to get back to a state of well-being, Kate missed out on downloading the wiring to self-regulate. Rather, Marion downloaded the wiring of vacillating between Brain State 3 and 4—when in 3 overthinking and when in 4 becoming anxious or even panicked. When she slipped to 5 and in a stress spiral, Marion reached for a cigarette or chocolates.

Ralph became a more active parent in the second year of life when setting limits with their active little girl became an issue. Kate was so physical that she was a handful, apt to run out in the street or take a tumble down the stairs. And though Kate was the light of Ralph's life, he was wired at Brain State 4, so his thoughts were extreme—everything was black and white. He indulged Kate with cookies and candy, spending far more on her than the family budget comfortably allowed. But then he would get so aggravated by her demands that he would punish her soundly. His repeated contact with her, particularly in emotionally charged moments when he was punishing her, wired into her emotional learning his most basic expectations about himself, which became wired into Kate as: *I am a bad person, I have no power,* and *Nobody will be there for me.* All the while Ralph adored his daughter and was doing the best he could do. These circuits tend to migrate from generation to generation.

Kate knew her parents loved for her, and as an adult, she could recite all the things they did for her. These memories were recorded in her conscious memory—the birthday parties, the cake with a doll planted in the middle, the strict enforcement of table manners. However, Kate's unconscious brain was on the watch for something else. It was looking for instructions on how to process life emotionally, and storing that information in the unconscious memory systems of the emotional brain. Kate would not remember any of the experiences she had before the age of three, for the prefrontal cortex would not have matured enough until then to effectively store conscious memories. All the while, the unconscious memory systems were soaking in information from Marion and Ralph's emotional brains.

Stress Has the Upper Hand

Even though Kate did well throughout high school and college, that basic software of how to process life was slightly ineffective, enough so that with the normal lumps and bumps of life her stress circuits became stronger. When she was in Brain States 3, 4, and especially 5, she didn't know how to get out of feeling bad, and the more time she spent in stress, the more those circuits became dominant. When she was at Brain State 3 she went numb. When she was at Brain State 4, she got anxious, bit her nails, and sometimes tried to talk with her dad. She loved and admired her dad, but most of the time he was locked away in his den, sipping scotch while watching the evening news. When she was at Brain State 5, like her mom, she ate sweets. So she developed circuits that tended to distance, and that distancing began to feel normal to her. She distanced from her mom, too, at about the age of 14. It was then that she realized that her mom couldn't just listen to her. She was way too anxious, and if Kate opened up, she would immediately start giving her advice in an attempt to control her.

Kate married George when she was 29, and she thought things would become easier. George's career was on the rise, and drug companies were good to their employees. They had a baby daughter who was perfect, all ten fingers and ten toes. But as mellow as life looked on the surface, Kate's stress circuits, one by one, were squashing her joy circuits. It wasn't any particular thing. Stress levels globally were up, and Kate, like most of us, was stressed out by the speed of change. Our hunter-gatherer ancestors equate sameness with safety, so our brains aren't naturally suited to chaos and overload. Kate was very focused on Ace, determined to raise her differently than she was raised. However, finding that sweet spot of being responsive to Ace, not distancing and being too harsh, or merging and being too permissive, was completely uncomfortable for her. She couldn't find that in-between connection, so she flip-flopped between indulging Ace with possessions and few rules, and being far too strict, even controlling with her. She sensed that she didn't have what it took to parent her daughter, and filled in the emotional holes by buying her expensive clothes, scads of shoes, and just about anything she anticipated that Ace might want. Ace did not learn to tolerate the normal pain of life and became overly sensitive to any small hurt. And these reactions made Kate even more anxious.

Ace was so indulged and emotionally deprived that she started acting out even more, as if to say to her parents, "How outrageous do I have to act to get you to give me the emotional connection and the safe limits I need?" At this point, Kate started popping pills, gorging on sweets, and packing on pounds around her waist. She couldn't control her sweet tooth, so she did the next best thing: she became attached to overexercising. It seemed to be her salvation, even though she was rapidly becoming dependent upon it. Miss a day at the gym? Never!

A Growing Complexity

Meanwhile George was climbing the corporate ladder and traveled more. Kate felt so alone, but most of her friends did, too, although nobody admitted it. Instead they complained about their husbands and kept busy, volleying from one external source of security to another throughout the day. Kate's life worked rather well in many ways, but beneath the surface, damage was being done. She was strengthening her stress circuits day by day, so her life was narrowing; she was whittling away at the joy circuits and her sense of peace inside. In a use-it-or-lose-it world of neural circuits, those homeostatic circuits were losing the contest for several reasons.

One was that life, as we age, tends to become more complex, requiring a greater capacity to self-regulate, to process stress effectively. Human development is somewhat like the development of computers. When personal computers were introduced, the operating systems were very simple. In 1977, the Apple II computer had 1 MHz processing speed and 4 KB of memory, and the applications they supported were rather simple. That processing speed worked pretty well. Then the applications became more complex, much the way life does, and so the processing speed of the operating system needed to ramp up. In fact, the average processing speed as of this writing is 1066 MHz and 2 GB of memory, perfect to support the more sophisticated programs. Life is like that. The infant has some rather basic applications, such as finding the spoon and putting it in her mouth, or reaching for mom's earrings and pulling on them. Not very complex activities, and not much of a processing speed is warranted. But as life goes on, the applications become more complex. Teenagers have to figure out what to wear and how to do their geometry homework. And adults negotiate more complexities, such as juggling work and home life, caring for sick children or parents, dealing with lost opportunities, burying dear friends, and passing away with grace.

If we don't "upgrade" our operating systems throughout the decades, enhancing our capacity to process daily life, these more demanding applications start making our system throw out error messages or even shut down completely. This is what happened for Kate. She started feeling as if she were spinning out of control—the fine lines around her eyes were turning into craters, and even with all of her exercising, she was growing a small tire of fat around her waist. Ace was so demanding and those mood swings were overwhelming. George was absent, locked away in the den, and she wondered if that flirtation he had with his marketing director—all right, it was an affair—was on again somehow.

Kate's brain state was getting stuck in stress, and she was popping more pills, indulging her sweet tooth, and feeling as if life was closing in on her. Who really cared about her, and what had she done with her life, anyway? And when would George get out of her hair and go back to work? When would Ace stop with her constant demands and sullen moods? Kate thought there must be something terribly defective about her, that she was a complete and utter failure. Sorry, no, a complete and utter, old-and-washed-up failure.

Actually, she was fine; the problem was those stress circuits. Because stress circuits are positive feedback loops, they don't have nice, neat shut-off valves the way joy circuits do. So the initial stressor, such as a disparaging look from George, which triggered an allostatic response, could easily send Kate into a stress spiral.

STRESS AMPLIFIERS

But what could it be about a glare that caused Kate to become so irrationally stressed? First of all, stressed states are inherently unbalanced, and they make really awful feelings, thoughts, and impulses crop up. We're apt to assume that we are vile individuals when we really listen to ourselves in this state, but everyone on earth has these same feelings, thoughts, and impulses when in stress. How do you think our ancestors survived? These reactions are actually protective in the right circumstances. The stress response, even though it is triggered by psychological stress, reads your state to be in terror of being eaten. It spontaneously induces unkind and extreme thoughts about yourself or others—or both. You are aggressive because you are afraid of being eaten! Even when your emotional set point shifts toward a state of balance, when stress dumps you into a stressed state, those cortisol-soaked responses remain extreme. Honoring that it is not us, just the chemical effects of stress hormones, can be liberating. You are responsible for your behaviors when in stress; however, avoiding judging yourself or analyzing what is wrong with you for those cortisol-tainted moments saves time and anguish.

Second, each episode after the first is a multi-layered experience—not just the simple triggering of the stress based on that singular experience—but one that is amplified by all similar experiences you have ever had. Not only are the most basic expectations of life—such as that you don't matter, can't trust anybody, don't have any power—aroused, but all the experiences from your entire life that are' similar. That is because of the nature of memory: it is state based. Your experiences are stored in a drawer-like fashion, so that when you are really happy, say in Brain State 1, the other happy memories are "hot" and easy to access. If you have a full drawer of happy memories, then when it's a sunny day, the sunshine sparks a happy mood and the circuits arouse other circuits stored on other sunny days and, there you are in a fabulous mood. The present experience is buoyed up by positive memories from the past, and it's so easy to sing a happy tune and be in love with your life. On the other hand, what if you have a lot of stressful experiences and those allostatic circuits are overflowing from the bottom two drawers in your brain? Not only are you the recipient of the shared extremes of the stress response, but emotional bombs from those now hot stress circuits start going off inside you, amplifying and extending your stress.

What's even more frightening about state-based memory is that it is unconscious, emotional memory with no source attribution, so you don't know right away—or ever—that this is an overreaction due to past experiences. And, you often have no idea what triggered it. The brain so favors overestimating threats that it allows these memories to be aroused by any state, emotion, sensation, or thought that even mildly resembles that past experience. A kindly co-worker who uses the same scent of deodorant as your rejecting father immediately draws your disdain. Going for a run increases your heart rate to the same level as when you were mugged, so running triggers a panic attack.

Without the tools to deal with both these current and past stresses, allostatic circuits can easily run over the homeostatic wires, and that's what occurred for Kate. Her emotional set point declined over time and instead of being wired at 2 or 3, she spent most moments of the day at Brain State 4. Kate used various ways to soothe and distract herself. Shopping was rewarding, and overexercise boosted her dopamine, and then there were pills and sweets. And like her mom, she found herself thinking way too much. She did the best that she could, but using these hedonic rewards did nothing to create joy in her life. They propped her up for the moment, and that helped.

Another reason that Kate's stress was amplified was that she did what we all do: she surrounded herself with people who were wired at the same brain state, as that felt familiar and therefore safe to her. What's fascinating to me about this brain state synchronicity is that it is so easy for you to identify the "other person" as somehow less evolved. A distancer connects with a merger, both equally separated from intimate connection. The person who slams doors and storms off in a huff finds someone who is depressed and passive and equal in brain states. The person who is lost in thoughts and considers that other person to be overly emotional is wired at about the same brain state as the person who is emotionally volatile.

In Kate's case, she and George, and even Ace were wired at about the same set point, even though their characteristics were wildly different. However, the more your circle of support is wired at a stressed state, the more influx of stress-related problems you have flowing into your emotional brain. If everyone is propping themselves up with maladaptive corrective actions, there will be a culture of chaos, shut downs, disconnections, and compromised health. That tendency toward brain state synchronicity, a throwback to ancestors who survived through tribal closeness and sameness, occurs not just in families or couples, but in communities and organizations all across the planet, over time as the culture evolves.

Who's on First?

After hitting the mall at 10:00 A.M. when the stores opened; trudging down the street to Bloomindale's; lunching at the glorious restaurant with the huge popovers, small demitasse cups of bullion, and tall flutes of champagne, Kate felt like her old self. Then she went home.

Kate waltzed into the house with four huge shopping bags—two from Bloomingdales and two from Neiman Marcus—and her true reward: a small bag with three tiny turquoise boxes tied with white satin ribbons, which held a diamond bracelet and two sets of earrings from Tiffany. She was definitely at 1 . . . or was it 5?

Then she saw George, blocking the door. George, who had gained ten pounds since his corporate departure, hovered over her like a bear, and he smelled like scotch, just the way her father had. Kate triggered a stress circuit. Instantly, she was furious. *How dare he block the door?* she thought. Her chest tightened, and her eyes turned steely. She glared at George and snarled, "YOU are in my way."

George just stared at her looking perturbed, but not saying a word.

Kate was incensed. Reflexively, she flung out her arms, still holding her shopping bags, in essence puffing up like an angry animal. And then in a fire-in-the-belly growl of a voice, she screamed, "Get out of my way. I said, GET OUT OF MY WAY!"

George sank, his chest caved in, and he looked at her for a long moment. Then he shook his head, and slowly he turned around, walking back to his den, as if in a trance.

For split second, Kate felt lost and even thought of scurrying away, running to her bedroom. But instead, she marched after him, following him step by step back toward his den. Suddenly, he turned around, slammed the door three inches from her face, and locked it tight.

At this point, from an emotional brain perspective, this entire encounter had almost nothing to do with George. Kate had triggered a stress circuit that was dousing her neocortex with cortisol. Normal extremes of emotions and thoughts fueled by stress flooded her being. Her own particular assortment of state-based memories caused emotional bombs to go off. And mirror neurons instantly replicated George's torrid emotional landscape. She was so overwhelmed with stress that she had no impulse control whatsoever. Immediately, Kate banged on the door with her fist. That didn't work. George didn't respond. So she ran to the kitchen, and got the meat tenderizing mallet and her heaviest frying pan. Then she raced back to the closed door.

How dare he lock her out!

Kate hauled off and whacked the door with the meat mallet. That felt great! Then she held up the frying pan, sensing that finally she had found the woman warrior in those circuits, like a cave women, she smacked the pan on the door. Crash! Ohhh, she needed that! Then Kate pounded the door with the meat mallet three more times for good measure, until she finally quit because her arm was getting sore. Then she tilted back her head and screamed like a banshee, right from her gut, "LET ME IN!"

Her words echoed through the big house, bouncing off the walls. Their property was large enough that none of the neighbors heard this out-of-control fight. Meanwhile, George was still on the other side of the door tucked away in his den. Even though Kate and George were both in Brain State 5, they had different styles of stressed-out behavior. When Kate was stressed out she was hyper-aroused, a bundle of passions, while George took the other route, dissociation. He took refuge in the den, in the safe surroundings of stacks of newspapers, his three computers, chips, scotch bottles, and candy corn. He settled back in his gray leather overstuffed chair and stared blithely at the large screen of his monitor. As Kate pounded metal objects on the door with every ounce of muscle she had, he wasn't really hearing her.

George's mind had turned to his red Porsche and wondering how he could get it back. Maybe he could luck out with day trading his stocks so that he had the extra cash to justify tracking that car down and forcing the new owner to give his baby back. He imagined putting on some Janis Joplin, the Grateful Dead, Paul Simon, and the Beatles, and driving up the coast, through Canada and Alaska. Maybe he'd take a ferry across to Russia. He'd never been to Russia and he imagined that soaring across the country in his beautiful red baby would be an experience like no other. Soon he was imagining finding his way back to a little bar in the Italian Riviera, maybe back to Portofino, and parking at the Albergo Splendido, the finest hotel in Italy. He could see himself there, sipping scotch, watching beautiful women dip into the aqua blue pool, and soaking in the pleasures of life for the remainder of his days.

Later, neither George nor Kate remembered what happened next, as cortisol at these doses tends to make you forgetful. The next morning George noticed that the scotch bottle was empty and three packages of his favorite candy corn were gone. On the other hand, Kate was off to the gym, fingering the new diamond bracelet around her wrist and thinking she looked pretty good for her age. These stress circuit were laid down in both of them before the age of three and even though the fight was not pleasant, arousing those old circuits can be quite comforting. They are so familiar, so old, that revisiting them is oddly satisfying.

Stress Adds Up over Time

What's one bad fight in the life of a marriage? The drama passes, Kate and George love one another, and life rolls along, but with each episode of stress there is a small but important price to pay, as the stress circuits become bolder and stronger, the joy circuits begin to fade out and compete less for arousal. All the characteristics of stressed states start to be wired into your psyche, so that it is easier and easier to be in that rut of the bad mood, the frustrating relationship, the bad habits, the repetitive thoughts, and the spiritual disconnection. It begins to be second nature, and since so many other people are wired at your same number, often Brain State 3, 4, or even 5, those ruts feels quite normal and even safe.

For a brain state to continue in this slow decline to an ever lower set point is easy. Without an anchor from early in life, staying attentive to your emotional state and switching it back to 1 never got wired in. So when stress starts to mount, that secure connection slips a bit. Then, when a few bad things happen—maybe the loss of a beloved pet or a job, or an illness—stress begins mounting even more. This accumulation of wear and tear on the body and mind is the stress load—or allostatic load—and it keeps wearing you down, adding to your stress until, at some point, the blinders come on. You are in what is called an allostatic state, a new set point of chronic stress. That state is outside the balanced homeostatic range, and the brain and body begin to defend it, and prefer it to a healthier one. The stress response that is protective begins to break down. Stress pioneer Bruce McEwen has shown that there are four types of allostatic load. One is when you have repeated "hits" of stress—first the divorce, then the money troubles, then the children acting out—and all the stress hormones cause damage by repeated activation. The second is due to lack of adaptation. Each morning when getting to work feels like the first day on the job: stressful. The third is due to the stress buzzer getting stuck on, frequently what occurs in response to trauma. And the last occurs when cortisol fails to respond adequately and other chemicals compensate by becoming overactivated.

As the stress response begins cannibalizing itself, stress symptoms start cropping up in several organ systems, and each stress symptom adds to the stress in the brain and more strongly wires the brain to stay stuck in that allostatic state. At this point, the greatest source of stress is the brain itself.

False Attachments Rise Up

Now stress is pouring into the brain from the whole range of stress symptoms: the backache that will not stop, the digestive problems, the diabetes, the weight gain, the hypertension. Yet all stress symptoms are not created equal—some are much stronger than others.

One type of stress symptom that accounts for much of the intractability of health problems is what we call external solutions. We separate them from the other stress symptoms because in health care they are often regarded as bad habits. For example Kate was attached to shopping. Was her spending just an ill-advised habit, something that a bit of advice could solve, or was it an external solution? If it was an external solution, then it fulfilled a survival need, was wired during stress, and was unlikely to be easily or quickly dismantled.

If you are not securely attached to yourself, you have nowhere to go when the going gets rough, so you naturally soothe and comfort in some other way. You can easily identify your external solutions by completing the sentence: I get my safety (love, nurturing, security) from _____. Securely attached adults get their safety from connecting to themselves, and if it is their belief, the deepest part of them, the spiritual. From that base of secure attachment, you can develop deeply intimate relationships that can sizzle with desire, comfort with emotional connection, and revel in loving companionship. Without that secure attachment, you are vulnerable to using emotions, thoughts, relationships, roles, and behaviors as external solutions.

In a way, that makes it easier, because if you are not getting your safety from yourself, as the primary pit stop, then it's a reasonable expectation that you will use external solutions. Some people dabble in them. Others move from excess to excess, and still others are solidly connected to one. Regardless, they are just external solutions, and what do they need? The knot of wires that attaches them to you needs unraveling, which you can certainly do, and you need to lift yourself out of that pit of stress and raise your brain state upward—slowly, but surely, until you are so securely attached to yourself that the drive for those false attachments fades.

Reward Centers Become Hijacked

If chronic stress persists for long enough, along with the external solutions, it may affect your reward circuitry. It can become tainted.

Stress causes imbalances in neurotransmitters, and in stress you can't access the eudonic rewards, so you are stuck with the default position of hedonic rewards. They cause abnormal highs and lows in neurotransmitters, which in turn create unstoppable drives for everything you know you shouldn't have. As Igor Mitrovic, neuroscientist and the scientific director of the institute that trains health professionals in EBT, has said, "The reward centers of humans are so easily corrupted by stress."

Repeated episodes of stress begin to burn out the neurotransmitter receptors sites in the brain, so you need higher and higher levels of artificial rewards—the sugary foods, the alcohol, or the nicotine—to feel good. In time, this adaptation results in needing the excess not to feel good, but to feel normal.

By this time, the reward circuitry is adaptable and because it is in stress, the prefrontal cortex is not overseeing the show. You are in terror, and then you reach for a substitute—for that cigarette, ice cream cone, or drug—and the brain remembers the experience. It can even create a similar neurotransmitter high, a substitution for the last one. This is why excesses that involve no ingestion or injection, such as gambling or pornography, can bring on a high.

ROLLING UP YOUR SLEEVES

What do you most need when you are wired for stress, attached to external solutions, with your reward pathways hijacked? You need a little compassion, a sense of humor, some support, and to roll up your sleeves and do some work. There's nothing wrong with you. You're just a little joy insufficient. You need your joy back, and that's just a matter of tearing down that wall of stress, breaking stress circuits, and finding your joy. In Chapter 6, you create a plan for becoming wired for joy.

Chapter 6

Getting Wired for Joy: Your Personal Plan

Let's go back to square one. George Valliant has written that all joyous states include happiness, but happiness does not necessarily include joy. Our goal is to use five simple tools to get the brain to a state of joy—the optimal state of well-being. You are training your brain to overcome the wild and wooly stress response in favor of the state that is your best shot of changing your destiny; that is, slowing or reversing the age-related increase in stress load so that you can live your best life.

The emerging understandings about brain states are throwing most researchers for a loop. We thought we could count on the number-one morbidity in the world—depression—to be genetic. We even found a gene that was thought to promote it. But now we've found that the underlying cause of depression is stress. What about gum disease? Stress. Cardiovascular disease and hypertension? Stress. We have wrongly thought that the epidemic of diabetes is just caused by all the sugar "those people" eat and how fat they get. But actually, the cause is stress. Stress is the underlying root that deteriorates every aspect of your health, ripping you from the lovely state of bliss.

However, we are at the beginning of what I believe is a paradigm shift in health care, moving from treating stress symptoms to treating the underlying cause—that is, the wiring that's provoking the stress. As this transition takes effect, we will have to resist the distraction of following the symptoms—the overeating, the anger, the depression. If Kate went to her physician after the little incident with the meat mallet, her doctor may well have given her some medication to reduce her anger, or he might have suggested psychotherapy to help her deal with her impulsivity.

The problem with this health-care model is that we become distracted trying to fight one symptom at a time rather than the stress that causes all the symptoms. Kate will become so distracted by her list of diagnoses that she will forget about attacking her stress circuits. If George goes to the doctor, she'll send him to AA meetings and tell him to cut out the candy and to start exercising, which of course he won't do, because he's wired at Brain State 4. Who exercises—other than compulsively—at Brain State 4? So he'll need medications for his cholesterol and his high blood pressure, and he'll have to get one of the monster-sized pill containers to keep track of all of them. Because the medications will blunt the symptoms, it may seem easier to just treat them rather than to bother becoming wired for joy. But by doing this, you do not change your destiny; you do not live your best life.

The five simple tools of EBT don't allow you to settle for anything less than a brain that brings out the very best in you, and you will methodically do the groundwork, using the tools to break your stress circuits and build joy circuits, one by one, rewiring the motherboard of your inner life.

Becoming Wired for Joy

So now that you know you have the capacity to change your destiny, how do you do it? You slow down and appreciate that rewiring the emotional brain is a practice, one that you use over time. You know that the solution is to acquire the tools to emotionally connect with yourself, and then, in your own time, begin using them.

At first you may think things such as, *what if I don't care about joy—I just want to get some relief from stress?* Or, *I don't even know if I want to be wired for joy.* That's just the effects of state-based memory.

If you are in stress, it will be almost impossible to imagine being in the flow of your joy. So use the skills at first just to move your brain to states of balance, and don't feel your joy until you are ready to do so. There is no rush!

You are embarking on a time of learning what the tools are and experimenting with them. If you are used to processing stress by thinking or doing, unplugging from those thoughts and actions, and plugging into your emotions is a huge step. It's stressful—stressful enough to send you to Brain State 5. So be gentle with yourself and know that just connecting with yourself and your brain state will have remarkable utility in your life. If you find you are ready to start using the tools and improving your state, then do that, instead.

Even if you decide to use the method in a way that rewires your brain, you will not always be at 1, but you will be emotionally connected to yourself more of the time. And you will be lovingly accepting that you are naturally in all five brain states in any given day. You are not bad when at 5 and good when at 1, but being more aware of your emotional state is a wonderful thing. You can observe yourself in Brain State 5 and say, "That's interesting. I really need to be at 5 now, and I will stay at 5 for as long as I need to." The last thing you want is to get in a tug of war with the emotional brain, asking it to change when it is not willing to. Besides, what the emotional brain needs most of all is connection, to be seen, heard, and felt; and that's what you are accomplishing each time to notice your emotional state, accept it, or even change it.

For most people it takes a while to trust the method. But the trust will come after you use it repeatedly and start seeing results. As you begin to explore using the method, consider what an amazing gift this is to yourself, to have the power to identify a stress circuit and begin to weaken it, and then another and another. The power to feel that surge of joy more of the time and the freedom to choose not to get to joy can be immensely freeing.

The tools are designed to be at your service, not to become another chore. So know from the start that you can give yourself complete permission to be as stressed as you choose to be. But also know that the tools are there to help you create a few more moments of joy than you had before. Move at your own pace. Some people come back to the method years after reading a book about it. All in due time.

Brain rewiring requires practice, and that means practicing the tools with others, as well as using them by yourself. The whole process is progressive, meaning that when you start it is hard to switch the brain to a state of peace and well-being, and when you do make the switch, it only lasts a moment.

As the brain begins to be rewired, it is easier to access some of the stress circuits that are stored early in life. More of the rewards of being at Brain State 1 start becoming natural, but that takes more time for people who have had early neglect, indulgence, or abuse, or for those who have had later losses, changes, or upsets. In the best of all worlds, using the method on your own would be all that would be needed for all people; however, that has not been my experience. So there are EBT courses that gently lead you through the training, gradually using the skills with more and more precision and depth, as well as EBT providers (health professionals to provide coaching and feedback and to facilitate EBT groups). Many EBT providers are therapists who use EBT for in-depth psychotherapy. Other health professionals, including physicians, nurses, social workers, nutritionists, and educators, use it for health promotion. All have completed professional training on the method and use the tools in their own lives.

Even then, the role of the EBT coach is to provide structure, advice, and support so that your daily use of the method moves you forward toward the rewards that are most important to you. Most of your practice is on your own, so you'll likely become highly effective at using the method during the wee hours of the morning, on the way home from work, or any time and any place you want to really see, hear, and feel yourself—to connect powerfully from within. As you use the skills over time, you may well find that they give you what you need: a change in your emotional set point so that you experience important benefits in every aspect of your life.

YOUR PERSONAL PATHWAY

Your next step is to create a personal plan for using the method. Let's begin by finding out what brain state you are wired at now, and what goals are most important to you. Then let's set out some reasonable expectations for how this practice will be for you and the support options available. The rest of the book will focus on the basics of the tools and the bridge between reading about the method and using it.

What Number Are You Wired at Now?

First assess your current wired brain state—the number that is your comfort zone—using the following questions. It is normal to be in all the states, but the more stressed your brain state, the more it is helpful to take it slowly, to be gentle with yourself, and to access support. The less stressed your brain state, the more success you will have in using the method more vigorously right from the start.

In the last month, how often have you experienced each of the five brain states? Circle the number that is true for you, and then total your score and identify what number you are wired at now. Then move to the next part of the plan, and determine what it will be like for you to start the training and how it will be to become wired at 1.

Brain State 1: Feeling Great!
Abstract thinking, joyous mood, intimate in relationships, spiritually connected, and optimal habits:

1 = Almost never
2 = Rarely
3 = Sometimes
4 = Often
5 = Almost always

Brain State 2: Feeling Good.
Concrete thinking, balanced mood, companionable in relationships, spiritually aware, and healthy habits:

    1 = Almost never
    2 = Rarely
    3 = Sometimes
    4 = Often
    5 = Almost always

Brain State 3: A Little Stressed.
Rigid thinking, mixed feelings, social in relationships, spiritually unaware, and moderate habits:

    1 = Almost always
    2 = Often
    3 = Sometimes
    4 = Rarely
    5 = Almost never

Brain State 4: Definitely Stressed.
Reactive thinking, unbalanced feelings, needy or distant in relationships, spiritually disconnected, and unhealthy habits:

    1 = Almost always
    2 = Often
    3 = Sometimes
    4 = Rarely
    5 = Almost never

Brain State 5: Stressed Out!
Irrational thinking, emotionally overwhelmed, merged or disengaged in relationships, lost or obsessed spiritually, and destructive habits:

    1 = Almost always
    2 = Often
    3 = Sometimes
    4 = Rarely
    5 = Almost never

Now total the scores from all your responses.

The range for this score is 5 to 25. Total score: _____

Score	The Number You Are Wired at Now
21–25	Brain State 1
18–20	Brain State 2
13–17	Brain State 3
9–12	Brain State 4
5–8	Brain State 5

How It Feels to Use the Tools

Wired at 1: Feeling Great!: If you are already wired at 1, learning these tools will amount to an emotional insurance policy ensuring that as new challenges arise you have a brain-based set of tools that will enable you to stay present in the moment, bounce back from stresses more rapidly, and deepen your capacity to access the powerful eudonic rewards. You will know your purpose in life and be more deeply aware of your rewards on a moment-to-moment basis.

Wired at 2: Feeling Good: If you are wired at 2, chances are you will find using these tools very interesting and helpful. You will learn how to spend more moments of the day at Brain State 1 and how to feel secure in being in all the states. You will be able to experience a great deal of stress but know the pathway back to a state of well-being. Chances are you will nab some stress circuits, weaken them, and find a new sense of peace, acceptance, and joy in your life. You may be able to start with using the tools frequently throughout the day and seeing favorable results within a few months.

Wired at 3: A Little Stressed: If you are wired at 3, you may wonder if you really want to be wired for joy or if feeling only a little stress isn't good enough. If you want these rewards, you may find that you can use the tools four to six times per day without much difficulty, but then forget to use them for a few days rather easily, too. It will be helpful for you to use EBT Kits (see Appendix B) and access a group for support but you may want to use the method on your own, instead. Be sure to identify which of the rewards is most meaningful to you, and then keep a vision of yourself with an abundance of that—or those—rewards. Focus on spending more moments of the day aware of your emotional state, securely connected to yourself, and more often than not getting to 1. Most people who are wired at 3 move to Brain State 2 within a few months and to Brain State 1 in less than a year, but everyone is different, and it takes as long as it takes.

Wired at 4: Definitely Stressed: If you are wired at 4, it may be challenging to imagine living life wired at 1 or 2, and you may want to focus on alleviating stress rather than creating joy. Go as slowly as you would like to go. You may have stress symptoms that are adding to your stress, so by all means use the tools to respond effectively to those symptoms by nabbing those stress circuits first. EBT Kits (see Appendix B) will provide you with step-by-step support in using the tools through the longer term, and an EBT coach can support you in weakening the circuits that cause you the most stress. You may find that you can use the tools 3 to 5 times per day and begin to see results within a short time. Some of the most important stress circuits that were wired early in life may take time to rewire, often a year or more, but as you rewire them you will feel a new level of peace and joy. Keep in mind that this is a practice, and enjoy more and more moments at 1.

Wired at 5: Stressed Out!: If you are wired at 5, these tools will provide a new sense of safety, and even learning about brain states may clarify why there has been so much stress in your life. Lovingly accepting yourself in all five states and not judging yourself is very important. EBT Kits (see Appendix B) will be helpful in guiding you through the process, learning how to use the tools to access the rewards, and off-load stress. These tools are stored in the emotional brain, so expect to first make remarkable progress, and then have periods where you forget to use the method and feel as if you are back to square one.

You are not. It is just that you are in Brain State 5, and it only seems that way. Return to the practice of using the tools and see yourself continue to transform. Using plenty of support, including one-on-one counseling, will help you advance more quickly. While being in an EBT group can be extremely rewarding, the most important thing is to start using the tools. Your emotional brain will not change more rapidly than it can, so develop a respect for it, knowing that the race is won by the tortoise not the hare. The journey takes as long as it takes, and each time you use the tools, you create small but important changes in your life.

What You Most Want

Now take a moment and consider what you most want from using these tools. Although the general goal of the method is to repeatedly lift your brain state to 1 and get in the groove of the chemical benefits it provides, you can focus the program to break specific stress circuits. This makes your program very individual. On your deathbed, if you look back and realize that you didn't have everything in life, what is the one thing you would regret not having? What external solution would you most want to live without? Take just a moment to identify what you most want to gain from this process.

The EBT Rewards

Sanctuary   Secure and peaceful from within.

Authenticity   Feeling whole and self-accepting; being genuine.

Vibrancy   Enjoying optimal health and vitality.

Integrity   Honoring your purpose and the ideals of importance to you.

Intimacy   Being close but separate from others.

Spirituality   Feeling connected to the grace and mystery of life.

Wired at 1   An abundance of all six rewards.

To reshape the wires in your brain takes discipline and persistence, as well as awareness of the brain dynamics that enable you to make this choice. We'll look at all of these in the remainder of the book, and we will focus on the tools themselves—how to use them and how they work. Right now, however, let's discuss how to begin rewiring circuits with the effectiveness required to create this transformation in your life.

THE PRECISE USE OF THE TOOLS

The emotional brain is a follower. It changes by the experiences you feed it, but it takes a passion and fervor to change it, coupled with making use the tools daily. In addition, be sure to use the tools just as they are described. These tools mirror the natural processing of the brain for optimal well-being, so following the rules to the letter is essential in order to bring you to your transformation.

Also, you must commit to being not only rigorous in using the tools well, but also vigorous in using them throughout the day. This is required in order to unseat the old way of processing stress, and put it in its place the circuits to securely connect with yourself, to lovingly accept yourself, and to have the choice of using the tools to switch the brain to a state of peace and well-being.

But be careful. Move only at a pace that is comfortable for you. If you completely unsettle your emotional brain, you'll end up at Brain State 5, and learning does not occur when you are overly stressed. Consider that every moment you are not using the tools, the old circuits—that outdated software—is still firing and wiring more strongly, and the longer you allow that, the more challenging and longer it will take to turn things around. Every moment that you use the tools, you are installing the new, preferred, updated processing software.

A New Purpose: Creating Moments of Joy

How do you know you are becoming wired for joy? You start spending more moments of the day in that groove. You wake up in the morning and know your purpose: to create joy in your life. For it is in that brain state that all the wasted efforts, manufactured problems, and mediocre moods vanish. What a way to live!

So begin by repeating to yourself throughout the day: *I am creating JOY in my life.* It starts with the word "I" to emphasize that you matter. Then it uses "create" showing you that you have the power to create. Then it continues with "JOY" because you are not settling for less. And finally, it concludes with "in my life," because your life matters.

This expectation is based on the primacy of process over outcome. If you don't make it your first priority to get to 1, the anxious brain will continue to take you down through the vagaries of stress symptoms. No matter what you do when you are in Brain State 5, it will not honor your best self. When you are at Brain State 1, most problems disappear, and for the ones that are left, you have the clarity, balance and passion to respond effectively.

Starting today, say "I am creating JOY in my life" out loud ten times per day. Use your tone of voice to make that experience more emotional and say it very loudly so that you can feel sensations in your body from listening to it. By doing this, it will be more apt to stick in your brain circuits. Say it to another person ten times. Say it to your pet ten times. Recite it in the shower ten times or when you are exercising. Keep saying it with a passionate commitment so that you know that you will do whatever it takes to become wired at 1 by spending more moments of the day in your joy.

The Humor of It All

This is definitely an adventure, and chances are that you'll laugh a lot as you use the tools. The emotional brain is a bit stubborn, but you have to love it. Don't be surprised if you use the tools smoothly for several days, and then work becomes busy, a friend is in need, and you completely forget to use them for two days. It is not just that you were busy. It was that the emotional brain prefers to change slowly, so if you nudge it too much it will simply stall.

It's not unusual to lose this book . . . really! Or to put it under your bed and forget that you ever read it. That's the emotional brain in action, protecting itself from those moments of joy that are disorienting and stressful. This is one of the reasons that it is so effective to use the method with others, because they are going to be hooting and laughing, too, and as you watch each other move your brain's set points and change in ways that are glorious and yet subtle, you will have a special connection with them, just as they will with you. Most EBT groups stay together regularly for several years, and then come back together at times, savoring the memories of the journey and sharing what's new in their lives.

As you begin using the tools, you're likely to notice a grin coming to your lips and if you're not laughing out loud, at least you'll be smiling to yourself—both at your amazing courage to rewire your brain and the secure feeling that you are addressing the root cause of most human suffering. You are supplying yourself with the wiring to move through stress, and back to that joyful place where you can give back, be of purpose, and use your talents and opportunities to their most powerful and rewarding effect.

CREATING JOY CIRCUITS

So how do you begin creating those joy circuits? You start right where you are, being aware of your emotional state, plugging into your emotions rather than your thoughts or actions. Periodically, you check in with yourself, taking "minute vacations" throughout the day to identify your number, your brain state. That emotional awareness mirrors the secure connection of two limbic brains, which is one of the greatest pleasures on earth. You feel loved—completely seen and heard. Of course you won't always do it, nor do you need to always use the tools, but the more you do, the more that connection will become wired into your brain and be spontaneous—at least more of the time.

Once you know your number, you can accept your state or change it. You can choose to use the tool that corresponds to that state, and by doing that you will deepen the joy tracks in your brain. Your brain will learn how to process each level of stress, each brain state. It will learn how to find harmony within more and more easily.

Begin to enjoy seeing yourself in stress, because becoming comfortable with stress, knowing you aren't bad or wrong, and that it won't last forever is part of self-acceptance and acceptance of the human condition. The point is not to be superglued at 1, but to be free to move among the states, and accept the times that you are resistant, overwhelmed, and miserable. It is your right to be in those states as often as you choose to be. Sometimes you stay in stress because you don't know how to get out or the situation is just plain stressful, and other times because it's delicious in its own way, as it is familiar.

It can be fascinating to spend a day watching your brain state change. For instance, you wake up in the morning feeling stressed out, numb, and desperate for a cup or two of coffee; and then you take a quick shower and feel sublime, if only for a moment. But in your rush to work, you get pulled over for speeding. You arrive late for the most important meeting of the day, having forgotten your briefcase and the financial reports crucial for your presentation. Perfect! You can figure out the number of your brain state and use the tool to lay down that perfect track that pops you back to Brain State 1.

At first the method is not easy. People who are used to getting As and doing everything perfectly get frustrated. This is the emotional brain. It's not cooperative and it changes in unpredictable ways, sometimes making spirals and leaps and bringing you "ah-ha" moments, and sometimes returning to its old ways, and needing focused practice of the tools to nudge it back to states of well-being.

Keep in mind that the emotional brain is loyal to your old wired state. It is not at all invested in you being wired at 1. It is your prefrontal cortex that is doing the work, repeatedly bringing the emotional brain around to that state of well-being. Your brain will not put up with such a primitive, fundamental change in short order. You have to work with your brain and understand its resistances and limitations, all the while keeping your commitment that you will do whatever it takes to feed your brain these new experiences, until it finds that joy is its new emotional home base, its new comfort zone, and prefers that state to the old stressed state.

CLEARING AWAY STRESS CIRCUITS

In a way, just focusing on spending more moments of the day aware of your brain state and switching it back to a more favorable state is how the method works. Neuroplasticity, the brain's capacity to change its structure and function in response to experiences, is competitive. When a stimulus arrives in the brain, circuits compete for arousal, and the most dominant circuit wins and fires. That firing strengthens the wiring, and the circuit that lost becomes weaker. This effect (what fires together wires together and what fires apart wires apart) is most pronounced in circuits that are opposite. Thus, the more moments of the day you spend in joy, the more you weaken stress circuits, along with strengthening the joy circuits. On the other hand, the more moments of the day you spend in stress, the more you weaken the joy circuits. However, getting to Brain State 1 requires weakening and breaking those allostatic circuits, which can be challenging.

We now know that emotional circuits are plastic, if we arouse an emotional circuit, drawing upon an emotional experience similar to the one that encoded it, the synapses—the links between the neurons—will become fluid and open to change. This is why being stressed—definitely stressed but not overwhelmed—is key to rewiring the emotional circuits. Once the circuit is open, the challenge is to respond to it differently, to feed it a different experience, which we do in EBT by using the tools. The circuit then begins to reconsolidate in a new form, as a homeostatic circuit.

How do you arouse these emotional circuits? Often there are enough stresses in normal daily life to take care of that for you. However, many past stresses are encoded in circuits that lie behind the veil of consciousness and require more creative ways to access them. We focus on various ways to arouse those circuits in the courses on the method, but one way to do this yourself is to begin to tell the story of your life, and when the telling of one incident triggers a stress response, you can use the tools to begin to rewire it. The changes that come from breaking circuits can be astonishing. You can find forgiveness for neglect or abuse, peace about a divorce or job loss. You can identify the roots of an addiction, or simply develop a cohesive narrative—a clear picture—of your life so far. That use of the tools actually erases a memory, and replaces it with one that is more accurate and constructive.

As you break stress circuits and build joy circuits, there is a need to fill in the blanks where there are cells that have died or withered. If your stress load is high, chances are that the major protectors of your consciousness, the prefrontal cortex and the hippocampus, have taken a few hits. Fortunately, the brain can create new neurons (the process called neurogenesis), but they have to be used in order for them to weave their way into the circuits of your brain. The formation of new neurons that are available to strengthen the frayed wiring in the brain is enhanced by the chemical brain-derived neurotropic factor (BDNF). BDNF serves as a fertilizer for new cell growth, as does living a life full of natural pleasures that increase rewards and decrease stress. Getting eight to nine hours of sleep; removing sugary, fatty foods from the house and replacing them with fruits and vegetables, whole grains, lean proteins, and low-fat dairy products; taking a therapeutic dose of a vitamin and mineral supplements plus omega-3 fatty acids; and getting at least 30 minutes of exercise daily helps cells latch on and fill in the blanks. These choices not only facilitate rewiring the brain, but also favor the genesis of new neurons that can fill in for the ones that stress caused to wither away or die.

Honoring the Mysteries of Our Lives

Keep in mind that some circuits are more challenging to alter than others, particularly those that are wired during the early years or during times of stress. Some can be rewired and some tend to remain, although weakened. So, what can you do about the ones that persist and simply will not go away? You can use other means of managing them. You can start by giving yourself some peace by appreciating that it is just a circuit. You are not alone. You are not the only one who has those strongly wired, maladaptive circuits living inside you, and then can put it on the shelf. We all have a shelf that is reserved for the mysteries of our lives, the hurts that we will never completely rewire, and the ones that we have used the tools on enough to extract many kernels of wisdom. That acceptance strengthens the intimacy you have with yourself and, thus, with others. You can forgive the spiritual and be at peace. You live with what is left, the part that you can neither accept nor heal. And you can have hope that you will one day find a way to address these circuits, as science advances more and more high-tech methods for rewiring will become available. That is the nature of life! So let's get started.

THE OPPORTUNITY TO WIRE ANOTHER

The woman in front of me had a profusion of curly ringlets, like blonde corkscrews, only frizzier, and she looked frazzled. Ace was eight and a half months pregnant and scared. Right next to her was her partner, Ronald, who looked much like I imagined him—lean from his mountain biking and rather professional, the young attorney.

Ronald spoke first, "We're living in an untenable situation now, but my position with the law firm starts next week, and we'll be moving into our own place before long. What worries me is the transition and what that will mean for the baby and for us. I have never been a parent before."

Ace broke in, "You don't have to parent this child. It's my problem."

Ronald paused and looked at me, not rolling his eyes, but almost. I turned to them both and said, "How may I be of help?"

Ace said, "I don't want to mess up my baby. I have no respect for my parents. My mother is a shopping addict and a gym rat and my dad is an alcoholic and a workaholic. I'm sick of them. I can't wait to get out of the house and be done with it."

I nodded and continued to listen.

Ace went on, "My parents were so ill-equipped to parent me and I don't want to make the mistakes they made." Ace was like all of us, hoping to do a good job with her baby and get it right, but what that would require is her being at 1 more of the time.

"Ace, you have a tremendous influence over your baby because 70 percent of genes have off and on switches that are influenced by the environment, and you are the primary environment."

"Good."

"Do you know what the single most important thing you can do for your baby is?"

"Take prenatal supplements and avoid alcohol and toxins?"

"Yes, that is very important. But what impacts the baby for life is your connection to yourself. You will download that into your baby's brain whether you mean to or not."

She looked at me, and then laughed. "That's unfortunate. I have an intensely horrible relationship with myself. I have no limits, and I know it, but I have no intention of changing. I can't change."

Ronald gave her a stern look.

"I've always done what I've wanted to do."

I was quiet.

Ronald said, "Ace, it's not all about you anymore."

"I don't need you to tell me that."

Ronald turned to me and said, "I want to learn the tools."

Ace said, "Me too."

"Great . . . let's begin."

Chapter 7

How to Score a Joy Point

The moments of pleasure you create are a formidable buffer to stress. In the method, we call them Joy Points, the feel-good moments derived from surges of neurotransmitters in your pleasure pathways. Those neurotransmitters light up the left prefrontal cortex—the part of the brain associated with feeling positive emotions and moving forward. At the very same time, they damp down the activation of the right prefrontal cortex, which is associated with negative emotions and withdrawal. Think of a Joy Point as a "freebee," something that is so quick and easy that you can sandwich it into a moment when you're stopped at a red light or waiting in the lobby of your dentist's office. It's like a short vacation from a work project or a quick emotional lift when everyone around you is stressed out. It's a blip on the screen of reward, but sometimes that blip is just what you need.

There is a certain thrill in knowing that wherever you are, even though this tool will not revise the foundation of your most basic expectations of life, you can use it to feel good . . . or great!

Even when faced with formidable stresses, if you can bring about the mental processes that invigorate your left prefrontal cortex, you can move forward through pain and come away from that with the abiding rewards of personal evolution. You will have stayed with yourself and overcome formidable challenges, and it wasn't so hard after all. You have sharpened your joy response—your personal skill at creating surges of pleasure in your body that wipe away the stresses of life.

When a stress comes your way, the most effective strategy is to say, "Oh, great. This means I need to muster an effective joy response. I can do that! What is the hard part? I have to use a mental practice. The reward? I have the security of knowing that I can do just about anything that I deem meaningful and right for me."

PLEASURE DAY BY DAY

A little while ago I was coming home from the city after a long workday, and noticed I was at Brain State 3. I was tired. I was a little stressed, and I could have used the tool for that state, but I didn't want to. I preferred to give myself a Joy Point, a freebee surge of pleasure. That would do the trick.

So I swung by Sunnyside Nursery, a locally owned business down the street from my house, as a way of giving myself a Joy Point. A Joy Point can be an experience or a thought that is rewarded with a spurt of dopamine. That burst of pleasure swamps the stress. That's why grown-ups enjoy pleasures like digging in the garden, listening to music, singing in the shower, taking time to pray, shooting hoops, and yelling at the top of your lungs when you score a basket. They all can work to boost joy.

At the nursery, I began walking through the rows of flowers, beholding their beauty, and wondering how many women over the ages had created surges of feel-good neurotransmitters by picking flowers. In short order, I felt that wave of pleasure in my body. At once, the stress of my day vanished. You can experience surges of joy, regardless of circumstance, just by bringing up a mental picture of a loving connection with yourself, with others, with nature, or with the spiritual. Learn to cultivate the habit of creating those surges. Some people call these small chemical orchestrations *surges of joy,* and others like the term *neuro hits,* but that chemical pulse has woven its way into the method. You use it for various purposes, including use in nearly all the tools, because the surge of dopamine it creates supports the strength of the synapses—the connections between neurons—as you fashion new circuits out of the old. Plus, used all alone, surges of joy make a definite addition to the quality of the day.

Why not start off your use of this method by making your own creative mix of joy surges before we move into how to use the tools of transformation?

Joy in the Body

Before you practice collecting a Joy Point, let's prepare by learning how to use the technique "Body at 1." There is a universal body posture that is a sign of positive emotions, usually with shoulders back, head up, perhaps even a smile on the face. You are energized, vibrant, intensely alive, and making magic in the world. You are your best, most powerful, and positive self. Those specific body patterns draw upon a sensory modality, *proprioception,* which provides feedback to the brain on the status of the body. Each time you arrange your body in that posture, and, if you like, facial expression, the brain interprets these signals as confirmation that you are in joy. Even if your mood is negative, shifting your body informs the brain that you are in joy.

This is just a small technique, but a powerful one, because it is brain-based and universal. You can even become quite stealthy in using it, such as during a tense meeting where everyone is standing around with their arms folded protectively across their chests and are emotionally closed down. If you assume Body at 1, your mood lightens and that can be contagious to others! What if you find yourself in the middle of a family meeting, where everyone is defensive and upset, and huddled around Brain State 4? You take a deep breath, assume Body at 1, and the positive emotional contagion begins!

119

Score a Joy Point

Brain Area: Prefrontal Cortex   **Target Circuits:** Emotional Brain
Time Required: 10 Seconds

Step	Purpose
1. Become Aware of Breathing	Easier access to emotions.
2. Assume Body at 1	Body sends brain message of well-being.
3. Create a Moment of Pleasure. Choose one:	Surge of Reward. Ease Stress.

- *Thought of a happy time*
- *Mental picture of loved one*
- *Words you most need to hear*
- *Compassion for self/others/all living beings*
- *A pleasurable sensation*

SCORING A JOY POINT

Now let's put Body at 1 together with some mental practices and create a chemical surge of pleasure in the body. In about ten seconds you can create that effect. Start by taking a deep nurturing breath or two and turn your attention to your body and your breathing. That shift of attention and that breathing ease stress, which makes it slightly easier to feel your joy.

Next assume Body at 1, to give your brain the message that you are in a state of well-being. Now bring to mind a thought or an image that brings you a wave of compassion. Most times it is a memory that evokes feelings of nurturing, love, and connection, which are all survival needs, and when you do something that supports survival, you are rewarded with a pulse of the feel-good neurotransmitter dopamine. If you like, create a bank of images and thoughts that predictably create surges of pleasure in your body. My bank includes the vision of my children's faces, memories of my mother when she would give me loving advice, and the thought of being in a very hot bath with oils and bubbles. Thinking of these memories and keeping them in your head will make them easily accessible when you might need one the most.

You can give yourself as many Joy Points as you want. They will break your stress and put a smile on your face, giving you momentary relief from the demands of life. How do you know it worked? Check if you can feel a relaxation response in your body: the damping down of the stress-based sympathetic nervous system and the ramping up of the relaxation response, the parasympathetic system. You will feel ripples of pleasure coursing through your body. That's a Joy Point!

Nobody knows you are collecting a moment of joy—feeling that chemical surge—but they will feel the shift in your presence, your calm energy. Practicing Joy Points is a great first step in using the tools, as they are interwoven. In fact, the last step of each tool is the creation of a Joy Point because that spurt of dopamine from a surge of joy consolidates the circuits after you've just been promoting, giving you a stronger rewiring effect with the same amount of effort.

MOVING TO A NEW SET POINT

I saw Kate weekly in the group, but this time she scheduled a one-on-one coaching session.

Kate explained, "I started this work to help George. At first it was just to try something new, but now it is for me. I have moved from being wired at 4 to wired at 3, but I have a long way to go. The reason I'm here is that nearly every connection I have is disintegrating before my eyes. I don't feel like spending the day at the gym. It's just the gym! It doesn't fascinate me anymore."

"Tell me more," I said.

"George is out of the worst of his funk, and Ace is about to have her baby and move to a new place with Ronald, and it seems like everyone is leaving me. George isn't leaving me, but I really don't know who he is anymore, so the marriage we had is coming to an end, and I don't know where it will go. I'm long past looking to my husband to define my life, but I really don't know what does define me."

"What a perfect time for you to become wired at 1."

"I kind of feel bad that my old attachments aren't satisfying me

121

anymore. What I most want from using the tools is sanctuary—I want that peace inside, to feel really secure, so I can finally just relax."

"This is part of the process, Kate. You are separating from the old attachments, strengthening the new ones, and tolerating uncertainty. It's like being mid-air when you let go of one trapeze but not yet grabbing hold of the next one."

"That's exactly how it is, and the worst part is that I don't even feel like shopping."

I said, "It doesn't do it for you anymore."

"Yes," she said. "Precisely, no zing . . ."

Remembering how toxic her home was when I first met her, I asked, "What's it like at home?"

"I don't really notice. Ace and Ronald are in their own worlds, but Ronald has become a good friend—he's so balanced. And as a couple they are ready to get their own place and be away from us old people. I've come to expect less of George. He's in such turmoil that his capacity for intimacy is lacking, but frankly, so is mine. We've lived that way a long time, but you know, I'm tired of judging him. I'm tired of judging myself. I'm tired of trying to control everyone."

Kate flopped back in the chair and sighed.

She said, "Last week, I missed two days at the gym. And I haven't weighed myself in two weeks. It doesn't feel like what I'm used to, but it feels really right."

"Kate, I just got a Joy Point listening to you."

She smiled, "That's progress, right?"

I nodded.

Then her face turned cloudy.

"I've been unwinding a knot of circuits—actually two of them—one from when my husband had an affair when Ace was 8 and another about my father. I always tried to please my Dad. As a kid I sensed that he liked me as a person, but he was so critical of my appearance. I felt like an object, that if I didn't look just right, then I was worthless. My stomach is turning over just thinking about it."

"What number are you at?"

She sighed, "I'm at 4."

I smiled. "A moment of opportunity . . ."

"I'm going to whack away at those circuits, use the tools on them once a day. I will feel some healing. Or reach acceptance—put it on the shelf of the mysteries of my life. Either way, I will have sanctuary, that peace. That's what I want most.

Then she smiled, and it wasn't the smile that I saw when I first met Kate. It was the smile of a woman who knew herself, and was beginning to accept her life, and cherish herself in a new way.

Chapter 8

Knowing Your Number

The first step in identifying the right tool to use to switch your brain from stress to joy is to know your brain state. Brain states are always flickering and changing if you are in balance, and when in stress they tend to get stuck, but you can change your state effectively if you use the right tool. That takes knowing your number.

That skill is called the Check In. Throughout the day, you use your prefrontal cortex to check in with your emotional brain and figure out your brain state. If you are in joy, you enjoy it, deepen it, and extend it with a tool. If you are not in joy, you use the corresponding tool to switch your state. You get to 1. Sometimes you prefer to simply accept your state. That's fine, too, for even a wave of acceptance helps strengthen joy circuits. Seeing and accepting yourself is at the essence of this method. But, on the other hand, why not get to 1?

One woman in a group at the university asked me, "Does that mean I can check out the rest of the time?" The more you use the tools, the more your wiring changes so that you are checked in nearly all the time. But remember, we're talking about changing the wires in the emotional brain. As you know, the brain does not welcome change. You must take time and practice—be persistent and patient— until you finally notice that you are checked in naturally, easily, and persistently. You are securely attached to the deepest part of yourself.

That is why developing a strong practice of using the Check In skill is so important. It is the reincarnation of your relationship with yourself—the mirroring of a secure attachment either you never had, or that was weakened or seemingly broken by the stresses of your life. Imbedded in that awareness of your breathing and experiencing that anchor in the present moment is the loving observation of yourself. It is the awareness of the larger truths of life, spirituality, and a sense of meaning beyond bounds. So this mental process of taking breaks throughout the day—this checking in—is both pragmatic and spiritual. It is pragmatic because it is a quick way to identify the number of the brain state you are in; it is spiritual because it gives you a process to establish a compassionate connection with the deepest parts of yourself, in which you sidestep indulgence or harsh criticism of yourself.

What's fascinating is that it is easy to be a loving observer when you happen to be in the balanced states, and it is really, really hard to maintain a loving stance toward yourself when in the tailspin of a stress response. However, you can try, and that is something worth striving for. Often, it helps to keep in mind that behind the harshly critical, confused, or outright indulgent voice associated with stress, is the kindest, most understanding voice you have ever known. It is in moments of stress—the moments that are akin to an emotional nosedive, the moments when even checking in is so challenging, the moments in which you forget to utilize the method—that you learn to "hear" your sublimely nurturing inner voice.

SWITCHING PROGRAMS

The first part of the Check In is to interrupt business as usual in the brain by pausing and taking a moment of silence, a "time out" from the rush of the day, to allow the brain's natural drive to connect begin to take hold. You are using this mental practice to change the software in your brain, weakening the wires of the old way, and strengthening the new. You are disempowering the old software and implementing a new way of doing things. So every time you check in and create that moment of relaxation and self-awareness, you will be closer to seeing important results. Even though you may start with a few Check Ins per day and work up to many, perhaps ten per day, finding a way to launch a new program is crucial.

You can remind yourself to check in via two methods. One is to use natural breaks in the day: when you awaken in the morning, are on your way to work, take restroom breaks, exercise, or eat. You can even use that moment just before you doze off in the evening. The other method is to use an outside reminder such as an alarm on your mobile device or computer, e-mail reminders, or simply a small pocket journal that you always keep on you—each time you feel it, it will remind you to check in. You can also get the iPhone app, called EBT, which not only reminds you to check in but also calculates your daily and weekly scores so you can chart your progress and the same automated tools are available on the method's Website.

Want to make this process even more fascinating? Find an EBT connection—someone else who is working with the tools—and contact them by phone or e-mail daily. It takes only 2 to 3 minutes to tell them how many Check Ins you did the day before and what you learned from them. That brief moment of fun and connection is satisfying and motivating.

THE ANATOMY OF A CHECK IN

After you've relaxed, made small but important shifts in your body, and observed yourself, then bring up a nurturing inner voice and ask, *What number am I?* The answers:

- **Brain State 1:** You feel great and balanced with positive feelings, such as ripples of pleasure or the glow of well-being in your body. Or if you feel a calm, energized sense of purpose, you are at 1.

- **Brain State 2:** If you feel balanced and good, aware of both your positive and negative feelings, and feel present in the moment, you are at 2.

- **Brain State 3:** If you are a little stressed, still feel somewhat secure in your connection to yourself, but either have no feelings at all (numb) or a fair intensity of negative feelings, you are at 3.

- **Brain State 4:** If you are definitely stressed, if you aren't sure what you expect or if your expectations are too harsh or too lenient, and if your negative feelings are rather intense, you are at 4.

- **Brain State 5:** If you feel overwhelmed and confused, unable to think clearly, panicked, deeply depressed, even lost, and feel like you have always been this way and will always be this way, then you are at 5 and in a full-blown stress response.

Check In

Brain Area: Prefrontal Cortex **Target Circuits:** Emotional Brain
Time Required: 10 Seconds

Step	Purpose
1. Become Aware of Breathing	Easier access to emotions.
2. Assume Body at 1	Body sends brain message of well-being.
3. Observe Yourself	Be mindful. Attune to yourself.
4. Ask, "What number am I?"	Identify your brain state.
1 = Feeling Great!	"Get to 1" or acceptance.
2 = Feeling Good	
3 = A Little Stressed	
4 = Definitely Stressed	
5 = Stressed Out!	

You may just want to accept your brain state because that loving acceptance and emotional connection can often bring you to a state of well-being. You are not fighting yourself. You are honoring your need to be in stress! However, using the tool that corresponds to that state gives you the power to shift it in predictable and profound ways.

This tone of acceptance pervades the method. You are not bad when you are at Brain State 5 and good when you are at Brain State 1. There are no bad numbers. There are people all across the planet who are in each of them right now. But why not get to 1? Each time you do, you strengthen the wiring that makes it easier to be at 1, creating that "groove" at your optimal state of being.

Notice that each time you use the Check In, you are moving forward in creating a new relationship with yourself that is accepting, loving, and powerful. Brain states are emotional states. We set no limits with emotions; after all, they are effective messengers to enable you to know what to expect and what your needs really are. However, it is safe to set no limits with feelings only if you are committed to setting limits with behavior. Let's say you are completely exhausted, frustrated beyond belief, and full of judgment. That's an emotional state, a brain state. Seeing yourself in Brain State 4 or 5, knowing that it is just a state, is an effective way to begin to move beyond that state. Being clear that, although you are in Brain State 4 and feel like judging someone or doing harm, you set limits with your behavior, you take action that minimizes harm.

The brain states of stress are normal and even adaptive. Life is stressful! Yet how do you know when you should nudge yourself to reach for the tools and use them, and when to accept that you are stressed and accept that you will allow yourself to be as stressed as you need to be?

If you tend to be really hard on yourself, it wise to purposely accept your state more often. You do not need to be perfect. Being at 1 all the time could create far too much stress. Acceptance of your emotional state is nurturing and powerful! That wave of unconditional love is just the needed medicine.

If you tend to be too easy on yourself, you may be apt to revel in stress when you are perfectly capable of nudging yourself slightly by using a tool. For you, it is highly effective and even necessary to reach for the tools when you don't want to. Asking yourself, *Why not get to 1?* can help. Otherwise, you might settle for being at Brain State 2 or 3 and miss out on your joy.

Finish your Check In with a wave of relaxation and reward. Regardless of whether you use a tool and get to 1 or accept your state without condition, by creating a surge of pleasure in your body, you strengthen the power of the experience. You more effectively rewire. You might say to yourself, *That was pretty good. I was really stressed and I took the initiative to ease that stress. Wow!"* Give yourself a Joy Point to reward yourself for having checked in and to consolidate a secure connection to yourself.

ACTION: A REAL CHECK IN!

Now let's put the mental processes together and follow an example of a completed Check In. Keep in mind that, with repeated practice, this becomes a ten-second process, but especially at first, it will take longer. What follows is the inner narrative of someone who is in the very early stages of trying to practice checking in.

"Amazing! Five hours just went by and I didn't check in. What is my problem? Did I just go numb or what? I'm too busy to do this. I have too many things to do. I don't have time to Check In. Oh, what's the use? I'll try it. I'm scared I can't do it. What if I come up with the wrong number? And if I figure out my number, who cares? Who really cares what my number is? I don't care. I've gone my whole life without knowing my number, and I'm too old to start now. All right, take a deep breath. I don't want to take deep breaths and feel. I LIKE thinking. I LOVE doing, and I don't have time for these emotional feelings. I need to start over: take a deep breath, exhale, inhale, exhale. Put my shoulders back and sit up a little. That feels better. I'm not going to change my facial expression. That's too weird. Now, can I observe myself? I'm not sure. Well, yes, I'm in this chair, in this office, and I'm definitely alive! Hmmmmm. I feel a wave of relaxation in my body, just a slight one. Maybe this will work. Now what is my number? I have NO IDEA what my number is. What is my number? I'm not at 1. I don't feel that good. I'm a little stressed, so I'm going to guess I am at 3. Okay, now I am going to accept my state. I accept that, for who I am, being a little stressed is about right. That makes sense. Now, I'm supposed to summon up a surge of pleasure. I can't think of anything pleasurable. Well, I can think of my dog. I love my dog. And I think I did a pretty good job. I feel a little tingle in my body. Good. I got my first Joy Point."

With practice, the Check In will sound something like this:

"Nice deep breath. Body at 1. Lovingly observe myself. What number am I? I'm pretty balanced, but I don't feel any positive emotions in my body. I'm at 2. I'll use a tool. (Uses the corresponding tool.) Yup, now I feel I'm at 1. I feel so glad that I see myself rewiring my brain, that I make sure I feel that surge of joy, that neuro hit of pleasure. Yes!"

IN THE BEGINNING

George had played with the tools on his mobile device, but he hadn't done the practice that begins to change the emotional brain. Instead he was thinking his way through this, which is completely ineffective, but that was what he needed to do. Everyone has his or her own process in getting started. Now it was time to get on with it.

George said, "I have started tracking my number."

"Great," I responded. "Have you decided what you want from using the tools?"

He nodded, "I want to be wired at 1. I told you that before. I want to cut down on those pill bottles."

"Is that all you want?"

He sighed, and said, "I want vibrancy, but really, I want more than that. I want to stop feeling bad in my gut. I want to stop feeling like a bad person."

"You talked before about feeling good inside—the reward of spiritual connection."

"That's what I want and I don't want to waste any more time. I want to be close to Kate. I love her. We first met when we were 28, and I didn't really know myself then. Nor did she. And it frustrates me that we have been living parallel lives for years."

131

I felt a wave of warmth for George. "I'm sorry you're so frustrated."

He looked at me, and then said, "Thanks."

I said, "When you were younger and didn't have the tools, it was impossible to be emotionally intimate with yourself, and that is the foundation for intimacy with others. When you have capacity to be loving and powerful in your connection to yourself, you can take on more stress, you can even tolerate the stress of being close to other people and feeling that tension. It's the tension of being close to someone without losing yourself. You can put up with that stress, because without it, other people are very irritating!"

George started laughing. It wasn't a chuckle, but a rolling kind of belly laugh that brought tears to his eyes and a mischievous little-boy grin on his face. He was now quite aglow with the merriment of it all, the reality that he was starting on a process and although he didn't know precisely where the changes would lead, he realized there was no going back." George cleared his throat, and then said, "What do I want? I want it all. I want to be wired at 1."

"That'll work!" I responded, feeling his elation. "George, the emotional brain is a follower. You need to use your prefrontal cortex to nudge it into shape, which means repeatedly rousing it out of its old way of operating."

"I can do that."

"How are you going to remind yourself to check in?"

"No question about it. I'm going to use technology."

"Using the EBT application on your phone?"

"That's right."

"Okay, use the mobile device, but none of these abrasive Check Ins. Figure out your number, but also ask the questions—kindly."

"I don't know what you're talking about."

"You are rewiring your relationship with yourself. That momentary vacation you take to check in is a time to bring in the mystical, to take a tiny moment to be aware of yourself, to feel connected to the deepest part of you."

"That's enough to send me to 5."

"That's fine. You'll learn the tool for Brain State 5 next week."

"I can see this is definitely a disruption in my life."

I smiled at him, enjoying his humor.

"I know," he continued. "That's the point."

"How many Check Ins are you shooting for each day?'

He looked at me and said, "Two."

I shook my head, "Not enough."

"Okay then. Four."

I sighed.

He said, "Five. But that's it!"

I smiled. "Fantastic."

With that, George got up, patted his cell phone, and headed out.

Chapter 9

The Tools of Transformation

You're ready to begin! You use your prefrontal cortex, the grand overseer of the emotional brain to tune into your state and identify it. Then you use the tools to switch your brain back to joy. Each of the five tools works only for the brain state that corresponds to it—that's why knowing your number is so important.

All these tools do one thing: they enable you to control your emotional brain and your brain state so that you spend more moments of the day in Brain State 1. And the more time you spend there, the sooner your emotional brain catches onto the idea, and establishes that as your emotional home base. When it does, the rewards flow and it all becomes easy. The tools use the natural processing of the brain to bring you back to Brain State 1, with the exception of the tool for Brain State 5, which sometimes switches you only from 5 to 4. But that's where you can do the important work of breaking old stress circuits, which, in turn, pops you to 1.

The tools are consistent with what a responsive parent does in each of these brain states. Because the job of parents is to support their child, the mandate of the tools is to find the quickest, easiest route through the brain from stress to joy. What does a responsive parent do when a child is in joy? Enjoy and extend it. In balance? Check feelings and needs. When the child is a little stressed? Elicit negative, and then positive, emotions. What about when stress mounts? Encourage talking about it, then expressing negative feelings, and finally finding a reasonable expectation to guide you through the upset, and to learn from. What about a full blown tantrum? Damage control of protection and reassurance that it will pass.

As it turns out, each of these tools is consistent with the nature of the brain in each state, too. When in joy, the relaxation response is activated and so is the reward circuitry. Let's deepen and extend that state. In balance, the brain naturally identifies feelings and needs, and in stress it needs to release some stress—some feelings—to return to a state of well-being. With more stress, the prefrontal cortex and emotional memories conspire to arouse past experiences of stress, narrowing the focus of that stress to the real upset emotions that, when expressed, point to unreasonable expectations, which can then be rewired. In a full-blown stress response, the reptilian brain is in charge, so quieting that circuit and stopping the unnecessary damage is the priority.

Again, these are natural processes, the way your brain most effectively processes stress in each of the five states. We'll focus on the tools in the order that is most effective to learn them. We'll begin with the tools for Brain States 5 and 3. These are easy tools, and by having both of them at your disposal when stress mounts, you can ease it effectively. After you learn these two tools, we'll move along to learn the Cycle Tool, the tool for Brain State 4. This tool is the powerhouse of the EBT method, and it is by using this tool that most people become hooked. This tool nabs and breaks those allostatic circuits, and the effective persistent use of this tool can be transformative. Last, you'll learn the tools for Brain States 2 and 1 to make it easier to stay in the groove of your joy.

The nature of these tools changes as you use them over time. At first they feel awkward, and they don't work very well and you do not trust that they will work. But as you settle into trusting the tools and anticipating the shift in your brain state, the process becomes easier and you learn a lot about yourself.. The best way is to begin is to expect very little to occur at first, and then enjoy the power of your prefrontal cortex to change your mood, not by chance, but because you are using mental processes that mirror just what it needs.

To access personal support in learning to use all the tools, visit the EBT Community Website (www.ebt.org). Your basic membership in the community is complimentary, and you'll have access to Web-based guides to help you use the five tools of EBT. Just establish a free membership, click on your number, type in your responses, and move from screen to screen for each of the tools. This service offers another option for accessing support and joining a community of individuals who are learning these skills, too.

THE FIVE STATES AND THE FIVE TOOLS		
Brain State	**Use This Tool**	**Effect**
1: Feeling Great!	Sanctuary Tool	Celebrate 1
2: Feeling Good	Feelings Check Tool	Get to 1
3: A Little Stressed	Emotional Housecleaning Tool	Get to 1
4: Definitely Stressed	Cycle Tool	Get to 1
5: Stressed Out!	Damage Control Tool	Get to 1 or 4

GETTING STARTED: CREATING AN EASY SAFETY NET

When you are stressed, a little or even a lot, the two tools in this section are very quick escapes from it, as they stop the rattling of that allostatic circuit. They are not difficult, and you can learn them straight away. If you aren't in Brain State 3 or 5 right now, just accept your state for the time being. Before long you will master the use of all the tools. We start with these because they give you a strong foundation for learning the other tools.

When at Brain State 5, Use the *Damage Control Tool*

To move from Brain State 5 to a better state, use the Damage Control Tool. This is a fabulous tool for bringing on a sense of security.

Once you know how Brain State 5 feels and how to apply this tool, you know that you can quiet that circuit and bring yourself some relief. You'll know how to stop the disconnection between the prefrontal cortex and the emotional brain, due to stress. You'll know how to calm the reptilian brain.

The Damage Control Tool consists of repeating three specific phrases over and over again until you feel a break in the spiral of stress you're feeling. The tool is very simple to use, by design, because when you're in a full-blown stress response, your thinking is not very complex. You need to keep it simple, and whether you say the words slowly like a chant or rapidly like peppering yourself with advice, you will use the same words.

All that the words do is remind you of the best strategies to use when the terror of Brain State 5 emerges. Because you naturally can be rather vicious when in survival mode—given that you are trying to not be eaten by a lion—you are full of judgment of yourself or others. So the first statement is, Do Not Judge (Myself or Others).

The next statement cautions you because harm often results from periods of intense stress when emotions, thoughts, and behaviors are naturally extreme and maladaptive, so the second statement is, Minimize Harm. This statement both acknowledges that there may be some harm (to assuage unproductive guilt about it), and cautions you to recall that you are responsible for your behavior (doing what you want to do when you want to do it, without regard for others or for yourself, isn't smart).

The last statement is, Know It Will Pass. After all, it's not me; it's just a wire. This is a brain state, and like all brain states, at some point it comes to an end. The time distortion of a stress response convinces you that the horrible way you feel right now will persist forever! This reminder helps you begin to believe that you are not in an endless black hole of stress. You are not going to die. You are going to lift yourself out of that state!

In Brain State 5,
Use the Damage Control Tool

Brain Area: Prefrontal Cortex **Target Circuits:** Emotional Brain (particularly Reptilian Brain)
Time Required: 2 to 5 minutes

Step	Purpose
1. Say, "Do Not Judge" (myself or others)	Create Secure Connection.
Say, "Minimize Harm"	Minimize Optional Pain.
Say, "Know It Will Pass"(It's just a wire!)	Lessen Time Warp of Stress.
2. Repeat (10 to 20+ times)	Break Stress Circuit and Create Joy Circuit.
3. Feel Surge of Joy ("Joy Point")	Strengthen Joy Circuit.

An example of someone using the Damage Control Tool sounds like this:

"Oh, I get it. This is not me, I'm at 5. It's just a wire! I need The Damage Control Tool.

Do Not Judge.
Minimize Harm.
Know It Will Pass.

Do Not Judge.
Minimize Harm.
Know It Will Pass.

Do Not Judge.
Minimize Harm.
Know It Will Pass."

What happens as you say this over and over again? The circuit calms, and then your brain state changes. Often it changes to Brain State 4, which is excellent, because you can then use the Cycle Tool to nab that circuit and begin to weaken and break it. Yet in the midst of your worst pain, often there is a ray of light, so be on the lookout—

sometimes under Brain State 5 is Brain State 1. The intense pain passes, and an intense joy appears. It's natural. Just be curious and after you say each statement, pause for a moment until it sinks in and you can feel in your body a slight emotional shift. Then continue with the next statement, and then pause again. I refer to this as the watch and wait. Your brain state may shift to 4, and that stress might turn into to joy, even a glimmer of it.

When at Brain State 3, Use the *Emotional Housecleaning Tool*

To move from Brain State 3 to Brain State 1, use the Emotional Housecleaning Tool. (This is my favorite tool.) You can let 'er rip and express your feelings, and in a matter of a few moments, you are at 1. Like all the tools, it works only when you are in the corresponding state, but most people are a little stressed quite often, so you'll have ample opportunity enjoy this tool!

This tool works so well because you are only a little stressed. The functioning of your prefrontal cortex is not completely hampered by excessive stress. You just need to offload a bit of stress. Stress is just excitations of neurons, and in Brain State 3, more neurons are activated. What is the best way to alleviate that stress? Express your emotions.

Notice as you use this tool that you'll have lots of feelings. If you were in Brain State 2, you wouldn't have a lot of feelings because the brain would be balanced and able to focus on one or two emotions and use those feelings to find your most important need. Not so, in Brain State 3. It's hard to know what your feelings are because your brain can't focus on just one, so the best strategy is to express them all, and the stress will abate.

Each time you begin using this tool, negative feelings will be strong. The brain errs on the side of being negative because these are feelings that keep you from being eaten by a lion. Start by expressing the negative feelings. What happens next? You feel strong positive feelings, which bring you back to Brain State 1. The tool involves expressing four negative feelings, and then four positive ones.

In Brain State 3,
Use the Emotional Housecleaning Tool

Brain Area: Prefrontal Cortex **Target Circuits:** Emotional Brain
Time Required: 1 minute

Step	Purpose
1. Express Negative Emotions *I feel angry that...* *I feel sad that...* *I feel afraid that...* *I feel guilty that...*	Release negative emotions.
2. Express Positive Emotions *I feel grateful that...* *I feel happy that...* *I feel secure that...* *I feel proud that...*	Increase awareness of positive emotions.
3. Feel Surge of Joy ("Joy Point")	Strengthen Joy Circuit.

The four negative feelings are anger, sadness, fear, and guilt. Those emotions comprise what we call the *natural flow of feelings*, because if you can feel your anger, not think it, but feel it in your body and express it, sadness naturally arises. If you can feel your sadness, then fear rises up, and once the fear has subsided, you become aware of what you contributed to the situation, and a feeling of remorse or guilt arises.

The next four feelings are the opposite of those negative feelings: grateful, happy, secure, and proud. Notice that we use "secure" rather than "hopeful" as the opposite of fear, because we are replicating a secure attachment through these skills and also because, when the brain is stuck in stress, the feeling of hope may not be balanced. It may be a false high, such as, "I hope I don't have to deal with reality."

Of the eight feelings, the ones that can be most challenging to experience are anger, guilt, and security.

- Many people are taught that it is not acceptable to be angry, but without a robust, "I feel angry" skill, sadness turns into depression.

- For some, feeling guilty seems dangerous because they think of it as shame. But guilt is one of the most important feelings because it enables you to identify what you could have done differently, so that you can learn from past experience, change, and grow.

- Feeling secure is difficult when those allostatic circuits create the sensation of being constantly on edge, as if you will lose it if one more thing happens. That's why this feeling is so important, because practicing feeling secure strengthens the wiring of security. After all, they are just wires, and you're in the business of adjusting them by strengthening some and breaking apart others.

To use the Emotional Housecleaning Tool, you don't have to decide what you feel ahead of time! You just say the words, and then watch the feelings arise—for example, "I feel angry that . . ." and then watch what comes into your mind to complete the sentence. Interesting! Now you go to the next feeling ("I feel sad that . . .") and notice what comes into your mind. You do the same for all eight of the feelings. What do you do if nothing comes to mind? You just go on to the next feeling. What do you do if you express a feeling and the feeling doesn't fade? (For instance, you say "I feel angry that . . ." over and over because you have so much of it?) Allow yourself to repeat stating the feeling, up to five times. After that, go on to the next feeling, even if you aren't completely ready to do that. Often if you allow one feeling to get stuck, it goes out of balance, and you are no longer in Brain State 3, but in Brain State 4 and need to use the Cycle Tool discussed in the following section.

Usually, when you complete the sentences, your responses are on completely different topics, so that you might be angry that you have to wash the dishes, sad that your partner is sick, afraid that you won't make the rent payment, and guilty that you forgot to feed that cat. If you find that all four of the negative feelings of Emotional Housecleaning are on the same topic, chances are that you are not in

Brain State 3, but in Brain State 4, which is perfect. Instead of nudging yourself to find the positive feelings—grateful, happy, secure, and proud—you go right into the Cycle Tool instead. Some people call that being at 3.5! However, because one of the two tools will be more effective, always err on the side of assuming you are in Brain State 4, as the Cycle Tool is the most powerful skill in the EBT method.

Here's a sample what it sounds like to use the Emotional Housecleaning Tool.

I feel angry . . . that I have so much paperwork to do.
I feel sad . . . that I have so much work to do.
I feel afraid . . . that I hurt my friend's feelings.
I feel guilty . . . that I didn't exercise today.
I feel grateful . . . for my children.
I feel happy . . . that I'm going to see my brother tonight.
I feel secure . . . that I am a good person.
I feel proud . . . that I cleaned up the kitchen.

After expressing your feelings, pause for a moment to reflect on what you just did and notice a wave of pleasure in your body to consolidate that circuit more strongly. Great!

NABBING STRESS CIRCUITS AND CREATING JOY CIRCUITS

Next, begin experimenting with the Cycle Tool, the tool that will enable you to nab a stress circuit, and then rewire it into a joy circuit. You can learn how to do deep, elegant cycles, and how to do quick cycles. Right now, start with quick cycles to enable your brain to feel comfortable with the process. You will see additional cycles in this book, but the point now is to trust the process and see for yourself that this magical tool can bring you a subtle relief from stress, and many times a profound shift back to joy that leaves you astonished and amazed at its power.

When at Brain State 4, Use the *Cycle Tool*

Start using this tool by talking about what is bothering you. Bring up what you are most stressed about, then state the facts about it. Those thoughts arouse emotional circuits that are the source of your stress. The stress may be reality-based, but most stress is due only partially to the situation. Most of it is due to an errant circuit that is amplifying the stress. The Cycle Tool enables you to identify that circuit and begin to wipe away the preexisting stress that it brings with it. As you express the feelings that ramp up from stating the facts, that circuit and its corresponding unreasonable expectation are exposed. What had been locked away in unconscious memory systems is now conscious. Now you can nab the circuit and reconsolidate it into a joy circuit of your choosing.

When you do a cycle, the emotional experience and the fact you have made an unconscious memory into a conscious one offer an important opportunity for rewiring. In that moment, the old circuits are open and stay open for up to six hours; however, they are most open to change directly after the cycle. During that time, once you have identified the offending circuit, you use a process called Grind In, which is repeating a thought that weakens or breaks that circuit. That same process is used to reinforce the continued weakening of the circuit, but the grinding in done in the middle of the emotional experience of the cycle is very powerful.

When you begin using this tool, you can bring up anything you are upset about, but it is best to bring up small upsets and hold off on arousing the circuits from deep hurts until you are adept at using this tool. As you start using this tool the two most important tips are 1) to be emotional, and 2) to keep using it until you *pop*. This is very important because if you don't feel the emotional shift, the rewiring has not occurred. A pop is the shutting of the fear circuit (the *amygdale*) and the activation of the reward circuitry in the emotional brain that is associated with the lighting up of the left prefrontal cortex.

The reason you express emotions during the cycle is that without feeling strong emotions, you are staying in the safety of being relatively balanced. In balance, the brain cannot open up the circuits that cause stress. So you must be willing to be upset to heal upsets. And you must stay in the cycle until you pop.

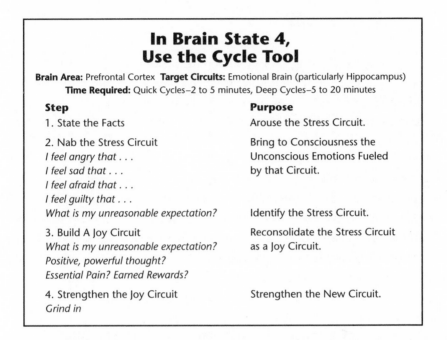

In Brain State 4, Use the Cycle Tool

Brain Area: Prefrontal Cortex **Target Circuits:** Emotional Brain (particularly Hippocampus)
Time Required: Quick Cycles–2 to 5 minutes, Deep Cycles–5 to 20 minutes

Step	Purpose
1. State the Facts	Arouse the Stress Circuit.
2. Nab the Stress Circuit *I feel angry that . . .* *I feel sad that . . .* *I feel afraid that . . .* *I feel guilty that . . .* *What is my unreasonable expectation?*	Bring to Consciousness the Unconscious Emotions Fueled by that Circuit. Identify the Stress Circuit.
3. Build A Joy Circuit *What is my unreasonable expectation?* *Positive, powerful thought?* *Essential Pain? Earned Rewards?*	Reconsolidate the Stress Circuit as a Joy Circuit.
4. Strengthen the Joy Circuit *Grind in*	Strengthen the New Circuit.

Since the brain rewards growth, you will not experience this pop unless you do something that helps you grow in a positive way. If you nab a stress circuit—an unreasonable expectation—and replace it with another unreasonable expectation that does not move you forward in the game of life, you will not pop. But if you replace it with an expectation that is reasonable and of meaning, you will feel that elation and power of a pop to Brain State 1. You not only feel great, but also know you've successfully rewired a circuit, or at least started the process.

In some ways, the EBT 5-point system is a backdrop for the astonishing power of the Cycle Tool. When you are in 5, the point is to calm the circuit enough to move to Brain State 4, so that you can begin to dismantle it. In Brain States 1, 2, and 3 you can lift your state up to 1 and strengthen the tracks in the brain that make you resilient.

However, those experiences are not as dramatic as the burst of healing that occurs when you do a cycle in Brain State 4.

Looking at an Example

Candy Cummings, an EBT Coach from San Diego, refers to those deep cycles about difficult hurts from the past as *Dumpster Cycles* and the ones about nuisances or small hurts as *Waste Basket Cycles*. Here is an example of a Waste Basket Cycle. You will see several Dumpster Cycles in the next chapters.

1. State the Facts: Everything in our department is a mess, because there are layoffs, and morale is down because everyone is expected to do more work on less pay. And I used to have support, and now I have to do all the administrative work myself, and lots of things are falling through the cracks.

2. Nab the Stress Circuit:

- *I feel angry that . . .* everything is changing. I hate that I have no support. I can't stand that what I have built in our department is unraveling.

- *I feel sad that . . .* our department is going downhill. I feel sad that things are changing.

- *I feel afraid that . . .* things are going to get worse. I feel afraid that these projects I've done are going to be taken away from me. I feel afraid that the whole department will fall apart.

- *I feel guilty that . . .* I am so upset about it. I feel guilty that I'm so stressed about it that I make things worse.

- *What is my unreasonable expectation?* (Under those feelings there is an unreasonable expectation, the circuit that is amplifying my stress.) It makes sense that I would be stressed about it because the expectation that is underlying those feelings is that I get my safety from my job going well.

3. Build a Joy Circuit:

- *What is my reasonable expectation?* I do not get my safety from my job. I get my safety from inside me. I get my safety from connecting with myself.

- *Positive, powerful thought?* (Typically, a negative, powerless thought immediately comes into mind. I will say to myself the opposite thought that is positive and powerful.) The negative thought is: I don't know how to do that. The positive powerful thought is: I am learning how to do that.

- *Essential pain?* (What is the hard part of following through, the truth about myself, or the human condition that I must face?) What is the essential pain of following through with that new reasonable expectation? I can't get attention for worrying about my work!

- *Earned reward?* (If I can accept that risk of the essential pain, and I do follow through, what will the payoff be?) The earned reward is: more peace inside. Sanctuary.

4. Strengthen the Joy Circuit: *Grind In* (What is the reasonable expectation that I want to grind in, to say right now because the circuits are open and ripe for change, and repeat ten times daily for a week or longer?) I get my safety from connecting with myself. (Repeating the Grind In at this time when the circuit is highly open to revision is expeditious!) Notice that it may change slightly as you state it so that it resonates with the deepest part of you.

I get my safety from connecting with myself.
I get my SAFETY from connecting with myself.
I get my safety from inside me.
I get my safety from within myself.
I get my safety from connecting with myself.
I get my safety from connecting with myself.
I get my safety from connecting with me.
I GET MY SAFETY from connecting with myself.
I get my SAFETY from CONNECTING WITH MYSELF!
I get my SAFETY from connecting with MYSELF!!!

When you complete a cycle, often you pop and are at 1. It can be a jubilant time, and if you have done a cycle with another person listening and being a loving presence (not interrupting or advising you, just listening to you), the emotion you feel is contagious: there is a limbic resonance, in which the emotional brains are echoing and amplifying the positive emotions. It is a very natural, very amazing high!

Consider trying out the tools, using the Web-based tools on the EBT Website or simply moving through the process as shown in the graphic. There will be more examples of cycles in the chapters that follow.

NOT SETTLING FOR MEDIOCRE

When you are at Brain States 1 or 2, you may say, "Give it a rest! Who needs to feel better?" Actually, you do, because unless you get to 1 at various moments of the day, the drives for unhealthy rewards ramp up. Plus it feels so great to be at 1! So let's look at the two last tools, the ones that are so very important to use to lift you up and over to your joy.

When at Brain State 2, Use the *Feelings Check*

This is the meat and potatoes of the tools, because imbedded in all the other tools is the awareness of feelings and needs. The Feelings Check tends to be underappreciated and underused, so I hope you get off to a good start by giving it your full measure of respect and attention. When you get to 2, that's not the time to slack off—do not settle for Brain State 2. Instead, use the Feelings Check and more often than not, simply using the brain as it is intended to be used when in balance—feeling feelings, identifying needs, and asking for support—will take you to 1.

This tool is extremely effective when you really are at Brain State 2. You know you are in Brain State 2 when you ask yourself the two questions of the tool: *How do I feel?* and *What do I need?* Finish off the Feelings Check Tool by asking yourself the question, *Do I need support?* to identify whether you want support from others in order to meet that need.

Asking these questions causes you to feel your emotions in your body; however, one strong feeling will arise in your consciousness, in your neocortical brain. If lots of feelings crop up, that means your brain is in more stress, and so the feelings are either exaggerated or diminished; that is, you are full of feelings that don't really point to what you need, or you find yourself curiously devoid of feelings. In those states, asking yourself how you feel and what you need is not effective. You end up saying, "Oh, I feel hungry—I need ice cream and cake," when you really may be tired or lonely, need some rest, or need a hug. So although the questions, "How do I feel?" and "What do I need?" are core questions, they elicit effective answers only when you are in Brain State 2.

What's a balanced feeling versus an unbalanced one? A balanced feeling can be either positive or negative, and yet it is not fueled by stress such that that it becomes distorted and persistent. For example, anger can be a very beneficial emotion, if there are things about which to be angry. Anger enables you to separate from others and feel your aloneness, the first step to coming to terms with your personal responsibility. Anger alerts you to dangerous situations, but you know

149

it is anger when you can feel the emotion, allow it to wash over you, and notice that it fades over time. If that anger has been mixed with sufficient stress, it will turn into hostility, and like all unbalanced, stress-infused emotions, it will become persistent and, quite often, not productive.

In a similar way, sadness is an important feeling, but when mixed with stress, it morphs into depression, self-pity, and powerlessness. Likewise, the productive emotion of fear, when doused with cortisol, turns into chronic worrying or panic attacks. Finally, guilt is a very productive feeling. It is the hallmark of personal evolution, the willingness to identify what you contributed to past experiences in order that you can make changes. Guilt is productive, but when mixed with stress, it turns into shame and the rejection of self, which breaks the secure attachment and sends you into a spiral of stress symptoms.

When you are in Brain State 2, the limbic brain is happily mixing input from thoughts, emotional memories, unconscious expectations, bodily messages, and sensory input. Acting as the brilliant calculator that it is, it sizes up the risks and rewards of each and settles into an emotion. That emotion is the message it sends to the neocortex, that alerts it to your needs. The strongest emotion is what your neocortex is looking for, because that points to your most important need. Meeting the most important need supports your survival. The way you survive is to pay attention to those emotional messages, but when you are in stress, you need to be aware that these messages about your emotions are imposters. Instead of following along with them or shutting them off, you need to learn how to switch your brain back to the state in which those messages are accurate.

The reason for identifying your accurate feelings is to point you to what you need. That need may be a logical need, such as, "I feel hungry. I need to eat." Or it might be, "I feel lonely. I need to call a friend." More often, it is an intuitive need. You ask yourself what you need and an idea of what that is arises from the activation of the circuits in your emotional brain. Whereas the logical need when you are hungry is to eat, the intuitive response reads your needs at a deeper, more accurate level. Perhaps you want to lose weight, so you say, "What do I need? To take a walk and wait a few minutes before eating." The logical need when you are in a meeting and feel really angry is to express your anger, but the intuitive response to the question, "What do I need?" may be to relax and get to Brain State 1.

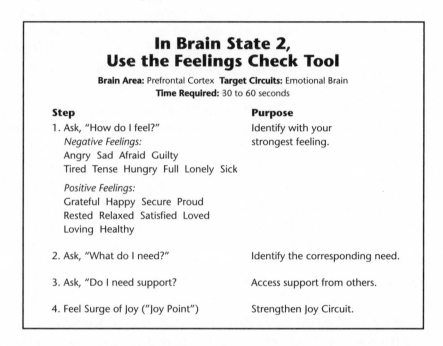

In Brain State 2, Use the Feelings Check Tool

Brain Area: Prefrontal Cortex **Target Circuits:** Emotional Brain
Time Required: 30 to 60 seconds

Step	Purpose
1. Ask, "How do I feel?" *Negative Feelings:* Angry Sad Afraid Guilty Tired Tense Hungry Full Lonely Sick *Positive Feelings:* Grateful Happy Secure Proud Rested Relaxed Satisfied Loved Loving Healthy	Identify with your strongest feeling.
2. Ask, "What do I need?"	Identify the corresponding need.
3. Ask, "Do I need support?	Access support from others.
4. Feel Surge of Joy ("Joy Point")	Strengthen Joy Circuit.

Another common need is just to feel the feelings and let them fade. If the feelings are balanced, you can devote yourself to them, allow them to wash over you, and they will naturally fade. It's a powerful experience! Of course, if you are in a stressed state, the feelings will just spin around, drag you down, or turn into obsessive, repetitive thinking. One important need is to check for what support you require from others, by asking yourself, *Do I need support?* Most people tend to go it alone, which cuts off opportunities for intimacy and means that more of the time your needs go unmet. So be sure to check what support you need from others.

After you do a Feelings Check, be sure to determine your state again, and more often than not, you'll find that you have nudged yourself to Brain State 1. That state of 1 is all about the rewards of connection, and by getting to that state, you fill yourself with elevated emotions, feelings associated with the greater meanings of life. The *vagal nerve*—the care-taking organ of kindness, play, affection, and caring—is activated, and with repeated activations, you train it to have elevated activity, taking you up and over to that Brain State of 1. That is your insurance policy of resistance to various external solutions, because you have trained your brain to experience that surge of natural rewards chase away the drives for excesses and false attachments. It is the smart way to be happy and healthy: getting into the groove of Brain State 1.

Notice that the feelings listed in the Feelings Check are not those typically considered to be emotions. They are feelings that pertain to all the basic needs of life. That is the role of emotions, so check for the whole range of them that signal survival needs. After you check, "How do I feel? What do I need? Do I need support?" take that extra few seconds to give yourself a Joy Point and reconsolidate the circuits more strongly.

When at Brain State 1, Use the *Sanctuary Tool*

A Joy Point gives you a momentary pleasure, which is important, but the Sanctuary Tool provides a rolling kind of spiritual joy that is more expansive and longer lasting. It brings up thoughts that trigger feelings associated with the long-term survival of the species and can be felt only when the brain is in supreme balance—essentially, in a state of perfect pitch.

All the tools can be used effectively only at the corresponding brain state, but there is no tool that more profoundly registers whether or not you are in its corresponding state than the Sanctuary Tool. It asks you to feel compassion for yourself, for others, and for all living beings. That's almost impossible when you are even a hair's breadth out of the brain state of 1. When I try to use the Sanctuary Tool when I am only in Brain State 2, my inner life rebels. Frankly, I don't feel compassion for myself, let alone for others. What about all living beings? That's hard to muster. Feel compassion for those people who are competing with me for my very survival? Forget it. So when you try out the Sanctuary Tool, if you find that you can't feel compassion, remember that it is not you, but your brain state. Human organisms err on the side of stress that pulls you from that lofty state for one reason: to favor your own survival.

There are three steps to the Sanctuary Tool. One is to mirror the evolutionary need for connection. Another is to create a level of compassionate connection, which creates a deep sense of peace and meaning. The last is to give yourself a Joy Point. All three act together to increase and extend the surge of neurotransmitters and the wiring, which makes for easy access and sustainability of the Brain State of 1.

Begin using the tools by lovingly observing yourself, really seeing yourself in this particular moment, and by so doing mirroring the loving connection between parent and child that is the basis for the imprinting of love and joy. Then shift your attention to your body, finding the place in your body where you experience safety. For me, it is my center, but for others it is in their chest or in the belly. In any case, access a mental picture of your choosing to connect to that safe place and plug into it. That secure attachment to the emotions in your body gives you an anchor within and connects you with an awareness of your inherent strength, goodness, and wisdom.

In Brain State 1,
Use the Sanctuary Tool

Brain Area: Prefrontal Cortex **Target Circuits:** Emotional Brain
Time Required: 20 to 30 Seconds

Step	Purpose
1. Lovingly Observe Yourself	Be mindful. Attune to yourself.
Connect to the Safe Place Within	Feel connected to yourself.
2. Feel Compassion for Yourself	Strengthen Joy Circuit.
Feel Compassion for Others	
Feel Compassion for All Living Beings	
3. Feel Surge of Joy ("Joy Point")	Strengthen Joy Circuit.

When you are ready, hear yourself say, "Feel compassion for myself." For a moment or two just enjoy the good feeling. If you find yourself fighting that, not wanting to feel compassion for yourself, use another tool to pop to 1 again. What if you have no compassion for yourself? That's just the activation or rumbling of those allostatic circuits. It's only a matter of time (and persistent use of the tools) until you break those circuits and can feel that depth of compassion for yourself, which is entirely natural and available to all. Just the way the stress circuits create a thick fog that obscures the loving-kindness that is within you, the joy circuits make that connection clear. They are just circuits, too, and you are building more of that kind, and breaking more of the unfortunate kind. It's a process, like renovating a house room by room, using the tools and building that sanctuary, that capacity for compassion within.

Next, continue by saying to yourself, "Feel compassion for others." Some people prefer to say those words, and then notice that one or two people come to mind. You can also form an image in your mind of one person you want to feel compassion for, and even imagine scooping up the warmth you've created inside and sending it out to that one person, chosen to receive warmth from within you. That mental picture of touching someone, with the kindness inside you, can create a surge of pleasure that is deep and wide. You are on a roll, because the arousal of circuits of compassion for yourself enhances the ease of arousing circuits of compassion for others, as that is the nature of emotional arousal (in the same way that having hatred toward another person arouses circuits of hatred toward yourself). You can use, to good effect, the natural tendency for like circuits to arouse like circuits.

Last, when you are ready, say to yourself, "Feel compassion for all living beings." Can you really feel compassion for all living beings? Is that normal, desirable, or even possible? It's a mental practice. It's the excitation of neurons that connect in a specific pattern. It is something you can choose to cultivate. Is it normal? No. When the brain is mired in stress, actually it's impossible, and since the average person is wired for stress, it is not common. Is it desirable? One might speculate that if you really felt compassion for your enemies, you would become their willing victims. Wouldn't all that gushing of good feelings take away your power and be dangerous for you?

In EBT, you set no limits with emotions; you honor all of them, positive or negative, balanced or unbalanced, as it is expeditious. Setting limits with emotions causes the whole elegant system of self-regulation in the brain to shut down. The brain is based on those emotions, and trusts that you know how to process them effectively, and processing them with exceptional finesse is what we are doing in EBT.

One of the reasons you can consider emotions to be safe in EBT is that you set limits with behavior. If a wild feeling is on a rampage, you tame it nicely, honoring the essence of its passion, but then you draw upon your neocortical mind to identify your behavioral response. You may feel intense compassion for someone, but choose not to be around him or her. You can have endless compassion for all living things, but decide to sign up for military service and go to war, or feel compassion for chickens and cows, but decide to be carnivorous and bite into a drumstick or savor a morsel of filet mignon. Although compassion influences behavior, it does not dictate it, making it safe to feel compassion, because you have limits!

Conversely, it's also an interesting activity to consider how you would limit your compassion. When you use this tool and ask yourself to feel compassion for all living things, where do you stop, who or what is excluded? Do you stop with the spider that's in the corner of the room, full of industry, weaving its web? Do you stop at the edges of your religion, or your city or your country? What about stopping with the people you like, and failing to have compassion for those you don't like. It's a fascinating activity to decide from whom you are going to withhold your compassion. (If doing that takes you to Brain State 4, using the tool for that state, the Cycle Tool, can be very effective in accessing the emotional recesses of your mind with respect to these ideas.)

It's really important not to push yourself too much to find that compassion for all living things, as compassion is an emotion, and it doesn't appear because of being forced. A more effective strategy is to play with these ideas and notice yourself cultivating an expansive sense of compassion that covers the planet with your emotions of loving-kindness.

Conclude using the Sanctuary Tool by creating one last surge of pleasure, which comes from a thought. Often I pause and reflect on the meaning of what I have just done, thinking that I am creating compassion in the world by creating it in myself. Whatever thought is most effective for you in creating that one last surge, you'll know it when you feel that warmth in your body, and notice that something strange has happened: Stress is gone. Problems vanish, and there is peace and boundless pleasure from within. It doesn't have to be a momentous experience. It may be felt as just a subtle wave, but you know its importance and how great it feels.

Practicing the Tools: Connections

As you begin using the tools you may go it alone, but you may also use them with others. We call that making a Community Connection and it figures into the process of learning. These tools are originally passed down—or not—from parent to child and are part of being intimate with others, so integrating practice with others into use of the tools can be rewarding and effective. Connecting with others to practice the tools is different from chatting with a friend, because one person just listens, without interrupting or giving advice. In essence, the person is a loving presence for the other, much like a respectful, loving parent or friend.

The other person uses the tool, typically does a cycle, and when the cycle is completed the person who was listening gives back by opening up about the sensations, thoughts, and emotions while listening. In a sense, the listener is returning the favor of being intimate. The listener is not parental and congratulatory, but instead shares what was going on inside—within the limits of what feels safe to say and they believe would be nurturing for the other person to hear.

Making That First Connection

Ronald took out a small pocket journal and put in on my desk, displaying his week's Check Ins, with the columns showing the number of Check Ins, the tools he used, and whether he got to Brain State 1 or simply accepted another state.

"I averaged eight Check Ins per day. My average brain state for the week was 3.2, and I did ten cycles this week. The only tool I didn't use is Damage Control. I scored 15 Joy Points, including the times I used the tools."

Ace began laughing, sitting next to him, propped up by pillows and seeming to relax under the weight of her baby, the movements of the baby in her womb, and the excitement of the impending birth. Ace piped up, "We're a perfect couple because the only state I recorded was 5, and the entire week I was using the Damage Control Tool. Now I'm feeling the opposite. I have been at 1 all day long."

"How many Check Ins did you do this week?" I inquired.

"I have no idea. I didn't really write them down, but I would say 3 or so a day, because Ronald was reminding me."

"What number are you now?"

Ace took a deep breath, put her shoulders back, and closed her eyes. A wave of peace came over her face, and then she opened her eyes and said, "I'm a 3."

"3?"

She nodded. "3. I wonder why I'm at 3?"

"Analyzing your state is not a solution."

"This is so unnatural."

"Precisely."

"Okay, I will use Emotional Housecleaning."

"Great. You might want to do a Community Connection, which means using the tools—usually the Cycle Tool—and asking another person to listen to you. Then you give a Connecting Message, sharing your own emotions, thoughts, or sensations that occurred while you were listening. Ronald, would you like to give it a try?"

"Sure, but why do I need to give her a Connecting Message?"

"It creates a supportive environment for one person to listen while the other uses these tools. Second, when someone is listening to you use the tools, the emotional intensity goes up, and that makes the tools have more impact on the wires."

"Okay, I can do that."

"That message is really powerful because you have shown Ace that you were willing to be moved by her work, and, even more, show that you were moved. It is far more intimate than merging with her, congratulating her, or acting as if you are her parent or teacher. And it avoids distancing, being emotionally removed."

Ace said, "My mother merges and tries to control me. My father distances, is fed up with me, and rejects me because I don't lie to him and tell him how wonderful he is. I would never want to be like him."

"What brain state are you at?"

"I am at 4 now. I just downgraded one notch by talking about my dad."

"Do you want to do a cycle, and Ronald, do you want to listen, and then give her a Connecting Message?"

He nodded. Ace did her first cycle.

"Do a brief cycle, nothing fancy. Just move through the questions. You'll be surprised how effective it is."

Ace nodded. "Just the facts. My dad is an awful person, and I can't stand being around him. He is so grumpy and negative, and I hate being around him."

I said, "If your feelings are strong, then go right into the Natural Flow of Feelings and nab that circuit."

She nodded, "I feel furious that he is such a jerk. I hate it that he is my father. I can't stand it that I have to put up with him. I feel sad that I don't like my dad. I feel sad that he is not a nice person. I feel sad that he is so sad. I feel afraid that I am mean to him. I feel afraid that I am a bad person. I feel guilty that I don't give him the benefit of the doubt."

"Great, Ace, now what is the unreasonable expectation under those feelings? Nab that stress circuit."

"My unreasonable expectation is that I expect him to be exactly the way I want him to be. I expect to have it my way. I expect to be in complete control of everyone."

"Fabulous. Is that reasonable?"

Ace looked down, and then laughed slightly, "No."

"Now build a joy circuit of your choosing. That will weaken the stress circuit."

"Okay, my reasonable expectation? I expect myself to begin to feel compassion for my dad, even if it is not easy for me."

"Positive powerful words?" I asked.

"I can do that."

"Essential pain? This is the wisdom learned, the kernel of truth in the cycle that enables you to move forward, learning in your life, evolving."

"The essential pain is that I can't always have it my way. I cannot be in complete control of everyone and everything."

"The earned reward?"

"I don't know."

"What would be worth accepting that you can't always have it your way? What is the reward of meaning, feeling whole and self-accepting? Authenticity?"

"Yes, that's it. The earned reward for me is authenticity."

"Did you pop? Are you at 1?"

Ace's face was radiant. I am totally convinced that beauty is about being at 1, and she was beautiful at that moment.

"What is your Grind In, Ace?"

"I need to grind in: I expect to begin to feel compassion for my dad. I expect myself to begin to feel compassion for my dad . . ."

As Ace finished her Grind In, Ronald spoke up.

He said, "When you were using the tool, I had a lump in my throat because I felt really happy to see you so loving. You inspired me to feel more compassion for your dad. Thank you."

I said, "Ace how was that for you to hear?"

"I loved it. I didn't know Ronald felt that way.

Then she turned to Ronald, "I love you. Thanks for being my partner."

Ronald smiled, and then collected their things, and the two of them, calm and loving, left.

Chapter 10

Break That Stress Circuit!

It was not going well for George—his face was puffy, with purple circles under his eyes, and he wore his big jacket, even though it was sweltering outside.

I said, "I'm happy to see you."

He slumped in the chair.

"How may I be of help?"

"I'm at 5. I've been at 5 all week."

"What is the tool for 5?"

"I don't give a rat's backside what tool is for 5. I'm at 5. Period."

I listened.

"Ace's is about to have the baby. Kate is still shopping all the time and at the gym, and I'm still nowhere."

"Do you want to use EBT?"

"Who said I didn't?"

"It's a wire. Wiring triggers brain states. Brain states get stuck. Are you having stress symptoms?"

"My blood pressure is up. My blood must be gushing with sugar. I haven't had a decent bowel movement in a week, and I have been going to the convenience store for white powdered sugar doughnuts, bags of them . . . and a quart of Johnny Walker."

"I'm worried. I need to check if you've seen your doctor."

"She will just give me drugs, and I'm sick of drugs."

"If you're stuck at 5, then you may need them."

He shook his head. "Everyone is leaving me. Ace is leaving. I play dominos with Ronald but soon he's going, and Kate and I . . . we're not close. Nobody that I used to work with returns my e-mails or texts. Why is everyone leaving me?"

"I don't know, George. What number are you?" I persisted.

"I don't give a ^$$% what number I am. Can't you see that I am hurting? Do I have to do this all by myself? What kind of a coach are you?"

"I'm not here to be your shrink."

He sat up, and then retorted, "I should say not."

We were both quiet. The heat came on and the only sound in the office was the noise of the fan turning. "Okay then, I'll do a cycle," he grumbled.

"You don't even know what a cycle is."

"You're right. I don't know if I even believe in it. But frankly, I'm desperate."

"I won't do a cycle with you unless you know what you are doing."

"Why not?"

"Because you are an engineer. You won't respect it unless you understand how it works."

"Laurel, you're hard to take."

Moving Out of Brain State 5

"I've been told that before. You're not a piece of cake either. Besides, you're not even at 4, so a cycle won't help."

"Okay, I'm at 5."

"I want to hear a robust Damage Control Tool."

"I can't remember how to do it."

"Take out your pocket reminder."

"I don't have one."

"Here," I said and I gave him a stack of them.

He looked down at the card.

"George, remind yourself that the vile feeling you have right now is not you. It's a wire!"

"Who says it's just a wire?"

"I do and you are miserable. You don't want to take pills. You don't want to see a shrink, so what is left?"

"You."

"Precisely."

He settled into his chair, "It's not me. It's a wire. What a stupid thing to say."

I shrugged, and cued him, "Now, Repeat: Do Not Judge. Minimize Harm. Know It Will Pass. Take an extra moment after each sentence, and let it sink in. Allow your brain to shift emotionally when it receives that message."

With eyes half closed, he started mumbling: "Do Not Judge. Minimize Harm. Know It Will Pass.

He wasn't pausing and letting it sink in, but it was a start.

"Do Not Judge. Minimize Harm. Know It Will Pass. Do Not Judge. Minimize Harm. Know It Will Pass. Do Not Judge. Minimize Harm. Know It Will Pass. Do Not Judge. Minimize Harm. Know It Will Pass. It's just a wire."

He sighed, "Okay, I'm at 4."

"Fine. Are you ready for some instruction?"

George bristled.

"I'll take that as a yes." George stared at the ground, and then nodded, without looking at me.

I said, "The way you feel right now is not you, but a stress circuit, and instead of being passive and ineffectual and allowing it to live inside of you for the rest of your days, you are going to break it."

"I don't believe you that I can break it."

"If you decide to goof off and not use the tool properly, you won't break it."

"I hear you," he said.

"Once a circuit is wired, anything close to what triggered it will arouse it again, and then it will become stronger, and even fewer similar things will arouse it, and then a whole range of different stimuli will arouse it, so that you are constantly getting triggered or feeling the aftereffects."

After a pause I continued, "The rumbling, the uneasiness, never being really comfortable in your own skin—that bad feeling you have? That's one of those circuits."

I nodded reassuringly. I wasn't sure he bought it, so I waited.

Revamping the Emotional Response

George said, "Okay, okay, I give up. It's a circuit."

"To break it, you can't use your engineering brain. You have to get the same stimulus, yet respond to it differently. You respond to the moment differently at every juncture throughout the whole cycle: emotions, thoughts, responses."

"Give me a break. It happens so quickly. It's emotional, for Christ sake!"

"George, it takes practicing the skill to learn how to break it."

"I'm trying to listen, but I don't know how to do it."

"First you have to arouse that circuit. It's emotional so you can't get at that circuit directly. Instead you have to think thoughts that are specific to what you are most stressed about right now and that arouses the circuits. You have to feel the emotions."

"I don't know what I am most stressed about."

"Yes you do. Just ask yourself, 'What am I most stressed about?'"

"Okay, okay, just the facts. I am most stressed about the fact that I spent 17 years of my life dragging myself to my job, working 14-hour days, traveling on business, preoccupied by my work, while I gained weight, drank too much, got one sickness after another, and my daughter was being babied by her mother, and my wife was spending all my money, and . . ."

"Good. You got the first phase of the stress circuit aroused, your emotions, but instead of doing what you normally do . . ."

"Going numb, drinking, playing on the computer, eating candy."

"You are going to do it the old fashioned way, the way the brain likes, which is to express your feelings."

"I *hate* feelings. If I start feeling, I am never going to stop. I'm going to go into this pit of emotions. I may never come out!"

"I doubt it."

George looked more miserable than before.

I suggested, "Just cough it up. Feel the anger in your belly, and then spit it out. Short choppy sentences: I FEEL ANGRY THAT . . . ! Your job is to get stressed enough so you're brain state is definitely 4, and the circuits in the emotional brain that are triggering that upset open up."

Circuits that are closed when we are just fine become fluid when we are in moderate stress. George's face turned bright red now, and I noticed that his chin was quivering slightly.

"I FEEL ANGRY!!!!!!!!!! I HATE those sons of bitches. I HATE it that they lied to me. I can't stand it that they screwed me over. I HATE it that I trusted them. I feel ANGRY that I didn't see it coming. I FEEL ANGRY that I . . . failed!"

After a pause he went right to sadness. "I feel sad that I am screwed up. I feel sad that the company deserted me. I feel sad that I am alone. I feel sad that my family is deserting me. I feel sad that I lost my job. I feel sad that I don't know what to do.

I said, "Stay in sadness until it becomes fear, which it naturally will."

"I feel afraid . . . afraid that I am a failure. I feel afraid that I caused all of this. I feel afraid that nothing will ever get better. I feel afraid that my life is over. I feel afraid everyone is leaving me. I feel afraid of being alone."

He could list the feelings, but the power of the method is not rooted in awareness of feelings, but emotional expression. After guilt he would naturally be aware of his part of it, and access his power to change.

I said, "Stay in fear until it becomes guilt."

George responded, "I feel guilty that I did it to myself. I feel guilty that I believed those jerks. I feel guilty that I trusted them. I feel guilty that I focused only on profits."

165

"George, that's the first phase of the stress circuit, the emotional phase, and you have just begun to break the wire by processing the emotion differently."

He just looked at me, still wondering if this would work.

A New Way of Processing Thoughts

"The second phase of the circuit is neocortical. The emotion has risen up to the neocortical mind, and you have the opportunity to nab the stress circuit. If you identify that circuit—that unreasonable expectation—you can break it and built in its place a circuit that carries you through stress back to a state of well-being. Basically, you're going to break that old circuit, because before, when it came to your expectations, you were thinking . . ."

"I didn't think. I just did. I just forged ahead."

"You couldn't really forge ahead because you had no map, and the expectations provide you with a map. Your stress caused the prefrontal cortex to function poorly, you had trouble concentrating, focusing, knowing your reasonable expectation."

"I'm having trouble following you."

"Precisely. Right now you have stirred up your feelings. You are right in the middle of your emotional brain. You used your thoughts to arouse just the emotions that are born of your unreasonable expectation. Knowing your feelings enables you to trace back to that unreasonable expectation. That expectation is formed only by repeated experience. It is unconscious."

George was agitated. "If it is unconscious, then what am I going to do about it?"

"George, you are doing just what you need to do. Trust the tools. Relax into them."

"I'm not relaxed!"

"What is your unreasonable expectation, the one that is under those feelings?"

"What is my unreasonable expectation? That the company should be my parent. I could give up control, and they would take care of me. My unreasonable expectation is I could trust them."

"You could trust them? Or you could not trust yourself?"

"I don't know."

"When the stress response hits, we go for safety wherever we can try to find it. If you do not have a secure connection to yourself to hold you, you do the best you can to grab some attempt at safety from somewhere else."

"My unreasonable expectation—the one that I lived by—was is that I get my safety from my company."

"Is that a reasonable expectation?"

He chuckled, an angry chuckle, more of a "humpf" sound, and shook his head no in answer to my question. George looked sad.

"You're in the second phase of the circuit. You have this amazing prefrontal cortex. You can use it to figure out a reasonable expectation that is right for you."

George coughed, and then said, "My reasonable expectation is that I should get my safety from trusting myself."

"George, when you say that reasonable expectation, it causes a stress response because you get your sense of safety from obeying the unconscious memories of the emotional brain. You're creating a revolution from within, so in order to calm the stress, you say some positive, powerful words. They are the opposite of the negative, powerless words that come into your mind."

"Right after I said that I should get my safety from trusting myself, what came into my mind is, 'I can't do that.'"

"So the opposite thought, the positive powerful thought is . . ."

He smiled, "I can do that!

The Circuit Breaks!

"Stay with it, George. Right now the synapses of the old circuit are wide open. That reasonable expectation is not yet burned in, because if it really were reasonable to the emotional brain, it would already be living there. It is on foreign territory, and in the most intimate way you must determine if it is really reasonable, for you.

He coughed again. He was stalling.

"George, EBT will not give you answers. YOU give yourself the answers. EBT just gives you the pathway to make those answers stick."

He coughed again.

I said, "To do that, identify what is the essential pain. What truth about the human condition or your life would you have to accept for your new expectation to replace the old one?

"I don't know."

"Trust yourself. Just take a deep breath and stay with it. You're doing great."

"You mean, what is the essential pain of following through with getting my safety from trusting myself? What will I have to face if I get my safety from trusting myself?"

He knit his brows and crossed his arms.

"I have to take responsibility for myself?"

I was quiet.

"I may not be trustworthy," he continued.

I was quiet.

"I have to grow up, not expect someone else to take care of me."

I looked down and waited.

"The essential pain of trusting myself is that I have to take care of myself, I can't drink, stay in my den, eat candy, and check out."

"And can you see the earned reward? Why would you separate from all that drinking, screen time, and candy, unless you had something better, in fact, MUCH better?"

He sighed, "Maybe I will get a job?"

I waited.

George blinked. He knew I wasn't going to buy that getting a job was enough to motivate him.

George shrugged. "You mean what do I *really* want?"

I looked him straight in the face. "Yes."

"Integrity. I want the reward of feeling proud about who I am."

George's face turned calm, peaceful, with an abiding sense of awe.

"That's what my company did not have, at least during the last years."

"How do you feel now, did you pop out of that 4 and up to 1?"

I knew he had. I could see it in his face, where the emotional brain is attached to the muscles and the skin, so that even relatively fleeting emotions are observed in changing facial expressions, which convey the inner life of the person.

"Yes! What do I do next in the cycle?"

Wiring an Effective Response

"This is the third part of the circuit, where you decide on a phrase that will both secure your new, reasonable expectation and bring you back to 1 in the future, so you can feel a surge of joy."

"I get my safety from inside me. I need to stop blaming the drug companies. They are just made up of people. Hell, I was part of it! And I need to stop doubting myself."

"Remember that circuit is open, when the synapses are loosened, so this is a highly effective time to repeat the new reasonable expectation to break that circuit. What phrase do you want to repeat, to grind in your new circuit?"

I waited, admiring that he was staying with it, in his first deep cycle.

"You want me to just repeat it?"

"Yes. Do you want to stand up and do it?"

He shook his head and self-consciously pulled his jacket tighter around himself.

"Do I have to repeat the new expectation?"

"No, it doesn't have to be those exact words, George. Trust yourself to come up with the best phrase, because what came out of that cycle is at the root of that old stress circuit and your capacity to break it."

"I get my safety from inside me," he began tentatively, but gaining in intensity.

"I get myself from inside me."

"I get my safety from me."

"I get my SAFETY from me."

"I get my SAFETY from ME."

"I get MY SAFETY from ME."

"I GET MY SAFETY FROM ME!!!"

"Do you want do more, George?"

He shook his head.

I gave him a Connecting Message: "George, when you were outraged with your company and the drug companies, my chest was tight and I felt your rage. When you said that you forgave them, I felt a deeper feeling, so much compassion for you . . . respect, really."

He took a deep breath and let out a long sigh. Then he smiled slightly, and said, "This stuff just might work after all."

The Ultimate: Reversing Stress Load

The final phase of using the method, the clearing away of those miscellaneous allostatic circuits, goes on for some time, as it is essential to prevent the amplification of stress and the consequent increase over time in stress load. Our goal with EBT is not just to stop the sensitization of the brain to stress from increasing, but to actually decrease it. In the 1980s, Dean Ornish conceived of the idea of heart disease reversal. The progression of heart disease, the build-up of atherosclerotic plaque in the arteries, is just one aspect of what allostatic load can do to your health. Bruce McEwen of Rockefeller University, a pioneer in stress research, has sought to measure a bevy of indices of that load such as high blood pressure, high blood glucose, and immune system suppression, but only recently have researchers begun to fathom *stress load reversal!*

George started using the method quite slowly, in part because his high stress load had him locked in Brain State 5. In that state, it took all his energy just to survive, and he really needed all his medications to prevent him from becoming even more tightly locked into a fixed state of stress and, frankly, to buy him the time to develop effective use of the tools. The best hope to stop his accelerated increase in stress load was to find a way to get even one cell of his body to be at Brain State 1, or even to get a brief glimpse that he could actually not be hemmed in by his stress load, so that emerging from his den was more of a possibility.

He had alienated so many people that there was really no one knocking on that door and hanging in there with him. I had tried nurturing George, but that had not helped him to use the tools with any frequency that would reverse the racing freight train of his stress symptoms. It made sense that love from outside couldn't penetrate that wall of allostatic circuits, for he wouldn't trust it, favoring discounting it or denying it instead. My goal was to help George reverse his allostatic load, and that would take raising his brain state toward 1, but stopping the train and beginning to turn it around is challenging.

When fixed at a stressed state, there are so many stress symptoms, not only the ones that are apparent but those that are underground, just waiting to surface. My hope was that something would break, one person in the family would get to 1 with enough frequency to seduce the other members into their vision of being at 1, and their emotional contagion would become infectious.

However, at this point, the family was in the phase of the training in which they are effective at clearing away the emotional clutter (the small wires that are important to clear away) but steering clear of the big ropes of wires. These ropes are the basic expectations so central that if brought to conscious awareness when their fixed state of stress was significant, they would shut them down, overwhelm them, and cause them to use every external solution they could get their hands on. The brain actually does a fair job of protecting you from rushing the process, because when a circuit it too stressful to heal, you go to Brain State 5, where you become hyperaroused or dissociated, to the point that you forget all about the wire.

CLEARING AWAY EMOTIONAL CLUTTER

This phase of the training that rewires stress circuits into joy circuits is productive in its own right, because healing takes a healthy brain, and during this time most people begin shaping up their lifestyle a bit, starting with decreasing their external solutions, and playing with the idea of using health care more effectively. From a brain standpoint, each time you break apart an allostatic wire and refurbish it into a homeostatic wire, you are enhancing your neural integration This integration is the way the circuits hold the brain together and keep it from splitting apart with feelings, thoughts, and responses that do not match up in a coherent and adaptive way. Each cycle completed that pops you to Brain State 1 enhances the coordination of the processes of life, so that it becomes even easier to rewire and to live a healthy life. So in this work, every use of the tools counts and, in time, it all begins to add up.

One of Kate's external solutions was merging, and she began to see the pattern in every last one of her relationships. She said: "I am a merger and I never knew it. I people please, rescue, and control. It makes me crazy and it's disrespectful to people, but I can't seem to stop doing it!"

"Would you like to do a cycle?" I said. At that moment, she was in the circle of an EBT group and since all of us tend to merge or distance—or both—not only would the other participants learn from her cycle, but also the emotional harmony in the room would likely skyrocket.

Kate said, "Sure."

We all settled into our chairs, as I coached Kate through her cycle and back to Brain State 1.

Kate took a deep breath and said, "Okay, just the facts. I don't know what to say other than I am a big fat merger. Get me within two feet of someone I love and I completely lose sight of my own feelings and needs, I have perfect x-ray vision of their feelings and needs, and I don't give a damn about anything other than shutting off their pain, getting them to like me, or finding a way to get them to do what I want them to do. It's awful."

"Are your feelings strong enough so that you want to cross that boundary from the 'Just the Facts' part into the feelings?"

Kate looked at me with a deer-in-the-headlights expression and mumbled, "Yes."

I said, "Start with, 'I feel angry that . . .' and don't overthink it. This is primitive. If the emotions don't come from your body, the cycle will not break that circuit. They can't come from your thoughts. They must be infused with emotion. I want to hear profanity, or if you prefer, extreme emotional intensity in whatever form works for you."

"I hate that I merge," she said, way too calmly.

No Emotional Gusto; No Wiring Change

"You don't sound like you're in Brain State 4 to me. Are you sure this is that upsetting to you?"

"What I'm most upset about is that I merge with George and want to control him, and then I distance and judge him. I do both."

"Would you like to focus your cycle on that?"

She nodded.

"I obsess about what he does, so that when he is in the house, his bad mood fills the place and I can't get anything done. Then I want to get out of the house, so I overdo exercise. And now my knee hurts. Sometimes I shop just to make myself feel better, and we really can't afford that. I'm tired of buying things I don't need anyway."

"Kate by keeping your Just the Facts on one topic, you will do a better job arousing the circuits that are fueling it. Try not to blend a lot of topics together."

"Okay, I'll stick to the topic of George. The facts are that in my relationship with George I merge with him and let his feelings overwhelm me, and then I say horrible things about him to myself and end up distancing, rejecting, and persecuting him. In some odd way I relish buying things, because I know how it gets under his skin and makes him madder. So the truth is that I merge and distance from my husband, and it is ruining my chances to keep my marriage together, to find a way to rekindle our love. I always blamed our relationship problems all on him. Now I think it is me."

Kate started her natural flow, "I hate it that I've spoiled our marriage. I can't stand it that I am such a *$^& merger. I hate it that merging is how I have survived. I hate it that I do it to my husband. I feel furious that I judge him. I HATE it that I persecute him. I can't stand it that I am such a mean person.

"I feel sad that I do that. I feel sad for him. I feel sad for me. I feel afraid that I cannot stop. I've been doing this since I was four years old, and I may never be able to stop. I feel guilty that I am so arrogant. I feel guilty that I haven't been intimate with him. I feel guilty that I haven't done my part to be loving toward George."

"What is the unreasonable expectation under those feelings?"

The Power and Safety of Limits

"My unreasonable expectation is that I would easily and naturally change a pattern that was wired before the age of 4." Then she started laughing. Others in the group visibly relaxed, perhaps seeing themselves in Kate's cycle.

Kate continued, "My reasonable expectation is that this will take time. I expect myself to begin to break the circuits of merging and distancing, and build the circuits that create intimacy in my life, particularly with George."

I said, "The limits cycle is your marching orders, the statement that you wire into your brain with the Grind In, but also the way you create power and safety in your life. The words you use to express it are very important, so please don't rush yourself. And will someone in the group volunteer to write down Kate's words?"

Kevin, a new participant in the group, a postdoctoral fellow in cancer research, raised his hand to volunteer, and then promptly pulled a yellow pad out of this briefcase and took out a pen to record the upcoming limits portion of her cycle.

"Your expectation has to be reasonable for who you are right now. Remember, even being aware of when you are merging and distancing is progress in breaking those wires."

Kate nodded and said, "I expect myself to do my best to be aware of when I am merging and distancing."

"Great! What negative, powerless words came into your mind as you said that?"

"I am too old to change."

"The positive, powerful words you can say that will weaken those wires?"

"I am NOT too old to change!"

"So what is the essential pain of following through with that new reasonable expectation?"

"I forgot what it was." Many people in the group smiled, having had that same "amnesia" experience during their own cycles.

Fortunately, Kevin was writing it down. The practice in EBT groups is for a person to write down the other participant's cycle, the part of the tool that starts with the expectation, because the stress is high enough that the brain may not recall the cycle. This is also why you have various ways to record cycles through Web-based tools and mobile devices. Remember this is one of the ways the limbic brain fights the change process: you forget the very words that reveal the allostatic circuit. Writing them down helps you hold onto them. Kevin read from his yellow pad, "You said, I expect myself to be aware of when I am merging and distancing."

"Oh, that's right. I expect myself to do the best I can to be aware of when I am merging and distancing. Positive powerful thought, I am NOT too old to do that. Now, what is the Essential Pain of that? I don't know."

"Kate, the essential pain could be many things. Check what resonates with you, what triggers a relaxation response: Maybe it's 'I must be present,' or 'I am not perfect,' or, 'It won't change overnight; it takes work.'"

"That's it," Kate said. "The essential pain is that it takes work."

She paused a moment, and the color came back into her face. She had popped to Brain State 1. That was her essential pain all right.

"The earned reward is intimacy, and even if that is not with George, I am creating the capacity to have intimacy in my life, to stop feeling so alone."

Breaking That Stress Circuit!

"What is your Grind In?" I prompted.

"I have to stop running around so much. I need to stop all this incessant exercising and shopping, and all the ways my mind gets caught up with thinking too much and calculating everything I do. I need to know my number, because if I am at 4 or 5, I KNOW I won't be aware and I KNOW that I will be merging or distancing. I just know that. So what do I really need? I need to get to 1, to stop fooling around with the tools, and start making getting to 1 my priority. I need to be aware when I am merging and distancing, but even more than that I need to get to 1."

"You won't do any of those things unless you break the stress circuit that is fueling those drives. It's emotional, Kate. Intending to change can't compete against survival drives. What is your Grind In?"

"What would help me the most is: I expect myself to get to 1, where I do not merge or distance."

"Is that what you want your Grind In to be?"

She was smiling now, exuberant, "Absolutely!"

"For the next few minutes—and up to six hours—that circuit is fluid. Do you want to say the Grind In with the group?"

"Yes!"

Kevin put down his yellow pad. Everyone got up and stood in the circle, with Body at 1, being a collective loving presence, as Kate did her Grind In, to reinforce it when the synapses of that circuit were most open.

She said, "I expect myself to get to 1, where I do not merge or distance.

"I expect myself to get to 1, where I do not merge or distance.
I EXPECT myself to get to 1, where I do not merge or distance.
I expect myself to get to 1, where I do NOT merge or distance.
I expect myself to get to 1, where I do not MERGE or distance.
I expect myself to GET TO 1, where I do not MERGE or DISTANCE.
I expect myself to GET TO 1, where I do not MERGE or DISTANCE."

Kate looked at me, "I need to do one more big one!

"I EXPECT myself to GET to 1 where I DO NOT MERGE OR DISTANCE!!!"

Kate was chipping away at those circuits one by one by one, clearing away the clutter, so that her brain set point would gradually improve, and perhaps even draw to a halt the age-related increase in stress load, and thus reverse the ravages of time.

Chapter 11

Personal Freedom

As you check in with yourself and switch your brain state, you may be aware that it is a gentle and nourishing practice. Day to day, you're traversing all the states and deftly using the tools to switch your state to a better one. Life is good!

Then, one day, you knock up against a circuit that will not budge. If your everyday stress circuits are slim strands, then these are thick cables. These wires are *survival circuits,* encoded when you were at Brain State 5, when you were in terror. Typically, these form early in life, when your prefrontal cortex had not developed to the point at which you could self-soothe, or in the ensuing years during moments of trauma.

These circuits form the emotional backbone for your external solutions—the smoking, the overeating, the raging, and all their substitutes—so they are important from a health perspective. What's more, they separate you from your joy.

WHAT'S A SURVIVAL CIRCUIT?

Let's take a moment to understand these circuits, and then explore how to rewire them. First of all, keep in mind that not all of them can be completely rewired. A veteran, for example, may have memories of combat that last a lifetime. An ex-smoker may have memory traces of the pleasure of lighting up for a long time. Yet by understanding the nature of these survival wires, you can sidestep being upset about being upset; that is, the secondary stress. Instead of judging yourself, you can appreciate that they are just wires. You can also understand the rationale for the tool that whittles away those circuits.

Because these circuits are encoded when you are at Brain State 5 —not 4—emotions are over-the-top intense. Thoughts are irrational. Behaviors are destructive. And each phase of the circuit is locked into your memory systems as if your life depends upon it, for that is what the brain perceives. It is going to do everything it can to be sure that given a remotely related stimulus, it will protect you by arousing the same whacked-out emotion, the identical idiotic expectation, and the very same irrational response.

This all happens in the blink of an eye, with the emotional response of terror being immediate—shutting down feelings or ratcheting them up to overwhelming proportions. That cortisol-dousing effectively separates you from all rationality during the second phase of the circuit, the neocortical-processing phase. On an unconscious level, you are responding to a fear of death. The prefrontal cortex is not functioning well, so you can't get your safety from emotionally connecting with yourself. Nor can you access it from having a reasonable expectation of hope and purpose. You are in a stress free fall, so you adapt quickly and find your safety from wherever your can—in the form of a feeling, thought, substance, or behavior. This reprieve effectively wires into the brain a maladaptive association between survival and something that has nothing to do with survival, such as "I get my safety from possessions" or "I get my love from overeating." At the moment, when you're desperately seeking relief from your stress free fall, your neurotransmitters are either excessively high or excessively low, both of which are associated with cravings and unstoppable drives. The third part of the circuit, the corrective action, must be quick and strong—quick because you are in terror and strong because stress causes imbalances in neurotransmitters. Those imbalances cause both urgency and pain. You make that response, get that immediate satisfaction and quick pain alleviation, and then you remember it! The speed and intensity of pleasure impacts your memory and adds to the addictive potential of your choices, which is why cocaine is more addictive than food. It delivers a stronger and quicker chemical reward, and the brain remembers being rewarded nicely, and then locks that memory into your circuits.

There, stored in your psyche, is a survival circuit, strong like a rope and primed to be activated again and again, becoming thicker and bristlier with each repetition. When you were in this free fall, this terror, it was this circuit that saved you from going into the abyss, completely overwhelmed by stress. So, you're attached to it. It is your lifeline, which means you need something very powerful to break it.

Keep in mind this is not just you but all humans, and over the eons, this capacity to unconsciously recall your reactions to moments of terror supported the survival of the species. And during that moment of terror and each time that circuit is re-aroused, you naturally block out the consequences of your actions. It's not that you are in denial, but in the moment of arousal, you are in Brain State 5. You simply cannot remember. You are responsible for your behavior, but your thinking is definitely tainted. The person who is 100 pounds overweight and in the middle of a food binge is shielded from thoughts about how the weight impacts diabetes. Long-term consequences are not on the radar when a lion of a survival circuit is chasing you.

Playing with Fire

What's more, in order to alter that wire, you must arouse it, and that requires being in the neighborhood of Brain State 5. It is not every person on the block who is willing to arouse strong negative emotions by choice. But that is what it takes to beat this survival circuit. You must feed it different experiences so it begins to wither. And the more you use the tools to resolve that stress and experience a burst of reward, the weaker the circuit becomes. The joy is when it gets so weak that the person who was superglued to overeating says, "I can't get my love from food. I get it from inside me!" Or even better, when the new circuit is wired so securely into the emotional brain that the drive to overeat turns off, the person loses weight, and he or she has no idea why.

You are dealing with survival circuits, and they are slippery. The challenge of arousing an emotional state, and then doing what is, in effect, a neurological U-turn, can cause stress, which is why in EBT we use a slow curve, chipping away at the circuits in a focused, intensive way, over time. One reason that people go into rehab is that the confined experience does facilitate facing their survival circuits. They have no other way out. But rehab that effectively rewires a particular behavior without rewiring the entire circuit can lead to addiction substitution. There is an emphasis on the third part of the circuit, changing the corrective response, but it turns out that the corrective response, in many cases, is the *least* powerful part of the circuit. The emotional processing and neocortical processing hold on, and they find a new third phase: the drinker becomes the overeater; the overeater becomes the overspender. In EBT, our form of "rehab" is the self-selected goal of being wired at 1, as that requires the peeling away of survival circuits for the ultimate purpose of meaning: they are getting in the way of your spiritual evolution, your joy.

EBT doesn't focus excessively on bashing those circuits. That would give them more power over you and could lead to the easy trap of organizing your life around ridding yourself of external solutions. Those external solutions already have enough power, let's not add to it! Instead, you create a vision of being wired at 1, with the whole range of eudonic rewards, feeling that boundless sense of power and grace. Those survival circuits can get in the way of your joy, so you do the logical thing and clear them away. You don't fuss about it or analyze it; you just do it, not because you should but as the ultimate gift to yourself.

Torch 'em!

Let's face it: we're dealing with fire here. Your survival circuits are hurting you. *They* are the problem, not you. So you have to torch them, and you have to do it in a way that is highly calculated, even elegant. To weaken your ties to external solutions, you will use a progressive version of the Cycle Tool. You must slow down the process, first identifying the unreasonable expectation, and then breaking the power of it *before* you lay down a new wire. Because the brain functions with the expectation that your very survival depends on this external solution, your attachment to that circuit is survival-based since, in a way, it was there for you when nothing else was. So you must mourn the loss of this expectation that has seemed to keep you safe for so long. If you try to lay down a reasonable expectation without first feeling the intense negative feelings of losing your old survival drive, you are apt to trigger a full-blown stress response. Instead, using this gentler approach, you can maintain a Brain State of 4, which is optimal for rewiring, as opposed to Brain State 5, in which it is challenging to sustain focused attention, and attention is the basis for rewiring. Any attempts to lay down a wire of joy without separating from the old expectation—amounting to doing that neurological U-turn—tends to feel superficial and inauthentic. So you must first negate the expectation that supports your external solution enough to weaken it, and then you can then begin the creation of joy wires.

This process is a tremendously empowering and nurturing act. Sure, you are going to arouse intense negative feelings, opening up the synapses of that survival wire. You know that arousing stress is essential to your success, opening up the circuit for a brief window of time in which it can be changed. Yet it is a nurturing practice, because you can control this emotionally charged event. Should you slip into Brain State 5, you can use the Damage Control Tool to calm that circuit enough so that you can open it up, and then reconsolidate it in the form of your choosing.

You're straddling the line here, because you want to arouse enough stress to open the wire but not so much that your prefrontal cortex is compromised, making it difficult to focus and concentrate enough to use the Cycle Tool effectively. To make these cycles more effective, it can help to surround yourself with warm support. Often, people do these cycles in community, with a trusted friend, or with an

EBT coach. Some people also log in to the EBT Internet community and use the tools together. The goal is to sustain a state that borders on Brain State 5, and use the tools repeatedly and effectively to break the old circuit and lay down a new, more effective wire.

USING THE CYCLE TOOL

Now let's look more closely at the powerful iteration of the Cycle Tool that will help you break free from the external solutions that get in the way of your health and happiness. This process starts with nabbing the circuit, slowly breaking it, and when the brain welcomes the opportunity, building a new joy circuit. This amounts to a neuroscience-based example of kill-them-with-kindness.

How to Switch from Stress to Joy		
Step	Purpose	Tool
1. See the Survival Circuit	Recognize the Unconscious Unreasonable Expectation.	Cycle Tool
2. Negate the Circuit	Mourn the Loss of that Unreasonable Expectation.	Grind In
3. Transform the Circuit	Marshal an Effective Joy Response that Breaks the Survival Circuit .	Cycle Tool

Step 1: See the Survival Circuit

If you feel stressed—more like 5 than 4—that's a good sign that a survival circuit is fluid and open to begin to rewire. You may need to calm that circuit down a little by using the Damage Control Tool to get to 4 and remind yourself that it is just a circuit, but so far so good.

Use the Cycle Tool, but keep in mind that your goal is really just to identify what that core survival circuit is all about. In a way, it is easier to find these expectations because they represent a survival drive. They emanate from your source of security being compromised. So to find that unreasonable expectation, you can ask "I get my safety/protection/love/nurturing from _____," and then see what comes up.

Often, when you find that unreasonable expectation responsible for your external solution, you are stunned. More often than not, this realization seems shocking, as if your emotional brain was playing tricks on you. Your brain is storing those awful, maladaptive circuits in your brain, without your even noticing! So the first step is to identify that survival circuit; that is, the unreasonable expectation.

When Ace came for a coaching session, she looked glum. She was uncharacteristically quiet but said she wanted to do a cycle. Ronald sat by her side, attentive, caring, and concerned.

Ace said, "I'm mean to people. I am mean to my mother. I'm mean to my dad. My parents tolerate it. Ronald is calling me on it, and . . ." Ace reached over and put her hand on Ronald's slacks and patted his knee. "I don't want to lose him. My external solution is rage, that's the emotion, and verbal abuse, that's the behavior."

"Can you put that together into one external solution, whatever name you want to call it?" I asked.

"Abusing others."

"Ace, any external solution is caused by being in terror, being at 5. It is a survival circuit. When your baby is born, she or he . . ."

Ronald spoke up, "We are having a son."

They caught one another's gaze and smiled.

"When *he* is born, he will be helpless, and his brain will be wired primarily by the two of you. So you do the best you can. Attune to him, meld your emotional minds and bring him back to 1, and the joy you share in that state will heal you both.

When you are at 5, you are like that little baby without a parent, with no overseer, and bereft of anyone whose emotional brain resonates with yours and ushers you back to well-being, so you do whatever you can to make you feel in balance. That's where that external solution came from."

"So you're saying these external solutions are infantile?"

"That's one way to think of it, but what I'm getting at is there are no judgments about external solutions. They were the fallback position, what we call a *survival circuit.* It was your better-than-nothing option, and it seemed to save your life at the time. That circuit was a way of keeping you from falling in that black hole of stress and being in terror that you would never come out."

Ace sat back in her chair and both Ronald and I did, too. We waited.

I reminded her, "The messier and more unbalanced the feelings, the easier it will be to clear away the stress. So let's begin: just the facts."

Ace said, "Just the facts. I abuse people. I feel so full of rage, and I light into them. I don't care about anyone else but me, and I don't care how the people I abuse feel. I am furious, and I let them have it."

I asked: "Natural flow of feelings?"

Ace nodded. "I feel furious that I am so mean. I hate it that I am such a loser. I can't stand that I act as if I am the only one on the earth who matters. I feel sad that I do this. I feel sad that I am so lazy. I feel sad that I can't control myself. I feel afraid I will lose the people I love. I feel afraid I will inflict this on my baby. I am afraid that Ronald will leave me. I feel guilty that I can't control myself."

"Great. Now nab that core survival circuit. What is your unreasonable expectation?"

"That I should be able to control myself? Of course I should be able to control myself. I'm NOT stupid!"

"Ace, don't set limits on emotions, only on behavior. This is the most challenging part of the cycle. See if you can find that circuit—the circuit that relates to your survival. I'll throw out some ideas, but only you know what it is."

She nodded her head.

"Look for emotions in your body. You'll feel a slight relaxation when the right one comes. That's because an expectation that is perfectly attuned to your needs has a calming effect. I want you to really see yourself—not the person you show to the world, but the person that is you, at your very core. Okay, listen to these possibilities: I get my control from raging at others. I get my safety from raging at others. I get my love from raging at others."

Ace said, "That's it. That's the one that resonates."

"That's a core circuit, a survival drive. All external solutions are based on survival drives. We desperately try to get love, nurturance, and safety from a thought, emotion, or behavior. It's stressful just to identify it, and can make you feel overwhelmed."

"That's how I feel. Exhausted!"

"Do you want to stop?"

"Yes."

"Okay, then we'll stop."

"But the circuits are open now, right?"

"Yes, your strong emotions opened the circuit."

"Then I want to go for it."

Step 2: Negate the Survival Circuit

The second step is to break that circuit. This is extremely important because that survival drive is so strong. Remember, these circuits were formed when you were in terror. They saved you from getting completely lost in stress. They are a safety net, and you can't rewire your brain without breaking this expectation down.

In Step 2, you take the unreasonable expectation and negate it. You don't try to lay down a joy wire, simply weaken the survival one. You use the negation of your unreasonable expectation as a Grind In. For example, if the unreasonable expectation is, "I get my nurturing from eating sweets," the Grind In would be, "I cannot get my nurturing from eating sweets." The Grind In for laying down a joy wire would be, "I get my nurturing from me." But with these survival circuits, this does not work. Instead, you feel that your survival depends on these wires, so you must first mourn the loss of them before you can set down a robust and authentic joy wire.

You will use the Grind In that you discover every day, saying it ten times, at least three times each day. Each repetition of the Grind In brings up strong feelings—anger, sadness, fear, and guilt—and the strategy is to feel those feelings and let them fade. Mourn the loss, pure and simple. This stage of the process should not be rushed, and it may take several weeks until you feel ready to move on to the next step in this process. And you will know when you are ready because saying your Grind In will lose its emotional charge. When you intentionally say it aloud, you are using conscious memory systems. Just like learning to ride a bike, when it is repeated often enough the brain prefers not to take its valuable attention to learning it, so it shifts it to unconscious memory. That is the basis for development. It takes a lot of focused concentration for a baby to learn to walk, but once it has been shifted to implicit memory, it is easy.

When you first grind in ("I get my safety from connecting to my emotions") it takes effort. Once it has been converted to implicit memory, you are ready for the next developmental learning. This is why EBT is a progressive process. First, you unplug from using external solutions and artificial pleasures as your lifeline, and then you gradually train the brain to connect with internal solutions and natural pleasures. These expectations are so foundational that many aspects of life may be favorably affected. However, the stress lingers somewhat, which is why the third part of the process is important.

Ace continued, "My Grind In would be: 'I get my love from me. I get my love from others.'"

I said, "That sounds logical to say the opposite, but it denies the primitive nature of these drives. When you go into a rage, how do you feel?"

"Like a monster."

"How scared do you feel?"

"Terrified. My mind turns blank, and afterward I can't even remember it."

"So it makes sense that a nice pleasant expectation—I get my love from me—would not begin to honor the ferocity of that terror and the emotional wallop of that circuit."

"Right, I see what you mean."

"So the next step is to negate the unreasonable expectation. By saying that to yourself, emotions will come up. Those emotions help break that circuit. In essence, you are grieving your loss."

"So how exactly do I grieve something that I can barely understand?"

"You don't make yourself feel. Instead you state the reasonable expectation, and the feelings will start rising up, and then you can process them."

"What is the expectation?"

"It is based on just what you said. You just negate it. The brain hates that, which is perfect. It's stressful, and it rewires. So the Grind In is: I CAN'T get my love from raging at others. Ready?"

Ace stood up. So did Ronald. I joined them.

Ace stood up straight with her shoulders back and said, "I can't get my love from raging at others."

"I CAN'T get my love from raging at others."

"I CAN'T get my love from raging at others."

Tears sprang to Ace's eyes. Her voice became low, choking back tears.

"I CAN'T get my love from raging at those I LOVE."

"Good, Ace, change the words so they ring true."

"I CAN'T get my love from raging at those I LOVE."

"I can't get my LOVE from RAGING at those I love."

"I CAN'T get my love from RAGING at those I LOVE."

"I CAN'T get my love from RAGING at those I LOVE."

"I CAN'T get my LOVE from RAGING at those I LOVE."

"I CAN NOT get MY LOVE from RAGING at those I LOVE."

"I CANNOT GET MY LOVE from RAGING at those I LOVE!"

Ace collapsed onto her chair, squirming back into the folds of it, and curling up in a ball, holding her stomach, her baby, and then Ronald tenderly wrapped his arm around her. I felt a wave of peace and hope in my body.

Ace left my office with the knowledge she needed to weaken the survival circuit that led to her rage. I wouldn't see her until three weeks later, when she felt that she was ready for the last step in this process.

Step 3: Transform the Survival Circuit

Once you have weakened the stress circuit, you can build another circuit that leads to a state of joy that begins to quash the stress circuit. It's important in this phase of the process that you pop your brain to 1, which takes more than the use of a hedonic reward. You must shut down the amygdale, and that takes overpowering it with the positive emotions from eudonic rewards.

Essentially, all you need to do is to use the Cycle Tool again. But in this case, you will work to build the joy circuit. If you were just dealing with a stress circuit, you could get away with using a hedonic reward. Instead, your goal is experiencing higher order pleasures. Nothing less will bring such a riveting and natural neurotransmitter spike.

Ace arrived alone, and said, "I'm feeling happier and more peaceful. Ronald and I are closer, and I want to do the third part of the rewiring."

"Great, just do a cycle about the same topic. This time it will be easier to pop to 1.

She nodded, "Just the facts. I have been grinding in that I can't get my love from raging at people I love, and I have found it less satisfying to rage. I still raged at my mother once, but it was rather tame. It feels uncomfortable not to have that outlet. It is so familiar. I have been doing it for a long time. I feel angry that I don't have that comfort of knowing I can rage. I feel angry that I can't do whatever I want to do. I feel angry that this work is ruining raging for me. I don't like it as much. I feel sad that I can't do whatever I want. I feel afraid that I will do it sometimes anyway. I feel guilty that part of me still likes to rage!"

"Great! Nab the circuit."

"My unreasonable expectation is that I can get my love by raging at people I love. My reasonable expectation is that I get my love from inside me. Positive and powerful. I have love inside. Essential pain? I can't do whatever I want when I want to. Earned reward?"

"Ace, you're doing great. Look for the reward of meaning that will take you up and over, and bring so much meaning and peace that it swamps the stress."

She sighed and was quiet for a moment.

"The essential pain is that I have to grow up. The earned reward is that I get to grow up. I get to be my own person—a loving person. That is what I want in my life. I want to be a loving person. I want love and closeness in my life."

As she said those words, tears sprang to her eyes.

I shook my head, smiling, feeling so happy for her. She was clearly ready to have a baby of her own.

Pulling the Plug

Many of these survival circuits attach you to external solutions, but often you think your external solution is the behavior. But any part of the circuit—the emotion, the thought, or the corrective response— can be your first love, your primary connection.

George came in for a session, but without being wrapped up in his jacket. Either he had lost it or he was feeling better. He was wearing a blue cotton shirt and pressed khaki slacks. His belly was visibly smaller, and his eyes looked brighter.

"George, you look healthier."

"I am healthier. I took all the sugar out of the house, I've cut back on the booze, and I went out to lunch today with an old buddy. Tomorrow, I have an interview with a start-up firm."

"A drug company?"

"No it's a start-up."

"A start-up company? What's the business involved with?"

I was bordering on crossing the line. It was none of my business what job area he was choosing.

"Well, it's kind of funny. I've decided to join Marvin Dodd, my old friend, at the nonprofit company he started to deal with the legal aspects of drug misuse. He said he could use a partner who knew the in's and out's of the industry."

"I thought you were doing cycles on forgiving the drug companies, that they were just people in stress and doing what naturally occurs in that state?"

191

"This is not revenge, Laurel. It is giving back, being of service, doing something . . ."

"Meaningful?"

"Yes, that's right."

"How may I help you?"

"I have been thinking about my external solutions, and I can't quite buy it that mine is alcohol or sugar or any of those things. I know they are an escape, but it is really a different kind of addiction. What keeps me safe is the feeling I have, just before I start the overeating or the drinking. That's where I get my security, even though it isn't really security. I'll be damned if I can find what that circuit is!"

I smiled. "I'm so glad you're here!"

"Okay, let's do it."

We both settled back in our chairs, and I felt a wave of compassion come over me that was directed at George. He was ready to work!

"What I want you to do, George, is to mentally bring up the last time you had a binge, the last time your reward centers started going haywire with your neurotransmitters, going both high and low, and you felt you just had to have that sugar or that scotch. Back up a bit, and take yourself through that experience, to the moment before the urge started ramping up. Chances are you'll find a survival circuit. The first step is to nab that circuit by doing a cycle."

He closed his eyes, and was silent for a moment, and then he charged forward, with a flourish, skipping stating the Just the Facts.

"I hate it that I am alone. I hate that Kate doesn't care about me. I hate that we are fighting. I can't stand that I am alone. I can't stand that I am so scared. I can't stand that Kate doesn't love me. I feel sad that I am alone. I feel afraid I am going to die. I feel afraid that Kate will hurt me. I feel afraid to exist. I feel guilty that I can't stop. I feel guilty that Kate doesn't love me. I feel guilty that I am so bad."

"Very nice. Now you can nab that stress circuit. What is the unreasonable expectation?"

"My unreasonable expectation is that I do not matter. I do not exist. I have no place in this world. I am nothing. I am nowhere."

"That may be a survival circuit, George, so the logical thing, the underlying unreasonable expectation, is what?"

He opened his eyes, obviously peering way down deep inside, and said flatly, "I get my safety from hiding."

I said, "What does hiding mean to you?"

"Hiding means going emotionally numb and separating from the moment. Separating from the pain of the moment."

We both paused, reeling from the emotional charge of the moment, and relishing it, too.

"I get my safety from being emotionally absent."

"Is that right, George?"

He nodded.

A Huge Old Rope

"Think about that for a moment, George. Imagine a circuit inside you that is like a rope, a huge, thick, bristly rope, and it was laid down at the age of . . ."

George said, "Three."

"And then things happened, and they re-aroused that rope-sized circuit, even though they weren't precisely the same situation, and the rope grew bigger and stronger . . ."

"Until it strangled me."

I sighed. He sighed. George stared off into space, perhaps thinking of all the ways that this circuit had hurt his life, his friendships, his marriage, his relationship with his daughter, and his relationship with himself.

"What do you want to do, George?"

"I want to break that rope."

He was ready to start the second part of the process, negating the unreasonable expectation, so that he could mourn the loss.

I smiled, "Shall we start?"

"How?"

"Grieve the loss of that false attachment. You can't get your safety from it anymore."

So George began: "I can't get my safety from being emotionally absent. I CAN'T get my safety from being emotionally absent. I CAN'T get my SAFETY from being emotionally ABSENT."

George was on his way to erasing one of his survival circuits, and by addressing these circuits, he would see important results more rapidly. In fact, the development of this new technology—erasing survival circuits—has boosted the power of the method considerably and made the Cycle Tool simpler to use. Once the reasonable expectation is clear, you can fast-forward to grinding it in.

If the circuit is deep and old enough, there is a fourth phase to the rewiring—maintenance. You must be aware that there are times when some sensation, thought, emotion, or behavior will arouse that circuit again. Sometimes it comes out the blue. The experience of a wartime memory, an early rejection, a personal betrayal, or a lost love can be encoded in a survival circuit that is re-aroused when you least expect it. That maintenance phase is straightforward: the circuit is aroused, and you see it for what it is, an old wire. You observe it, use a Grind In to further dismantle it, and send it on its way, at least for that moment. Maybe it will be triggered again and maybe it will not be. Wires do that sometimes.

One by one, George and members of his family whittled away at those survival circuits, and as they did they noticed something new in their lives. It was hard to put a finger on, but perhaps it was a fresh sense of being free.

Chapter 12

Joy No Matter What

The whole family was making good progress, moving along using the tools, but they weren't yet wired for well-being. They would have to keep on whacking away at those stress circuits and, instead of settling for Brain State 2 or 3, reach for another tool and boost themselves up to that state of 1.

And this will be the same in your process. You reach for 1. At first you won't quite fully understand how the tools work, and you'll find them foreign and clumsy. But with practice and devotion to the process, you'll notice that they work. You can identify your brain state, reach for a tool, and switch to this state of 1. One moment, you'll feel resentful, a little nasty, and on edge, and then all of a sudden, you have boundless compassion. And then you'll do it again, and again, and again, and each time it will be easier and easier.

One of the first things that many people notice when they start exploring the ideas of the method is that judgments begin falling by the wayside. After all, those negative qualities naturally emanate from stressed-out brain states, and everyone is in Brain State 5 some of the time. It is not logical to judge others—or yourself. You learn that although it feels objectively bad to be in stress, it has a silver lining. In that state, the synapses are most fluid, and you can more easily rewire. Stress offers you a moment of opportunity. Moreover, you start to see that stress and joy really are bedfellows. It's just that one kicks the other one out. It is not the objective measure of stress or joy that determines your brain state, but the faceoff between them.

When you settle for hedonic pleasures alone, you are at a disadvantage, for these rewards are not as formidable as eudonic pleasures—they don't stand up to pain as effectively. Yet if you rewire those stress circuits (and, more often than not, come up with an earned reward that is of a nature of being good), the brain starts to transform. It gets that you are all about doing your messy best to be of service—not just to you or even to your neighbor, but it gets the idea that you are in the flow of the survival of the species.

There are benefits to that, because the chemical burst of power and resilience that comes from those rewards can ease your stress. That's the ticket. You have not only learned about joy on a conscious level, but also rewired your emotional brain with unconscious expectations of hope and purpose. These expectations hold you in such a state of focused energy—all renewable—that you move through stress, even laugh at it. The power of the earned reward surmounts the stress of the essential pain so that you can feel joy, no matter what your circumstances.

That is your power in life, for you can steer your own ship. You have learned how to use your brain effectively and experience joy more of the time. You have become a wizard of stress processing, and can trust the capacity of your prefrontal cortex to arouse surges of pleasure that swamp the misery, drudgery, and humiliations of a normal life. You can come out of the muck feeling good . . . even great. The unconscious drives fueled by the quiet pursuit of sanctuary, authenticity, vibrancy, integrity, intimacy, and spirituality make mincemeat of stress. It doesn't have a chance!

That's not to say that stress won't be woven into your daily life and reward you in certain ways. The closer you get to being wired for joy, the more the ghosts of past stresses start whispering in your ear, things like, "Other people can be joyful, but not me." "I don't deserve to be *that* happy." "If I ever really got joyful, something or someone will come along and ruin it all, stealing my joy from me." And there are moments when misery is your most nurturing state. I still like being miserable at times, and I would not want to deny myself that right. However, once the emotional clutter has been cleared away, the attachments to external solutions weakened, and those tracks in the brain from each of the states to joy deepened, something strange often occurs.

You get your joy back. You are in the groove and those stressed-out states pass quickly most of the time. It is all so easy, and you look back on the journey and wish you had recorded it all. It's the greatest story ever told—those cycles, and the times you nabbed that stress circuit, broke down those wires—demolished them! Right at the center of that circuit you found a kernel of wisdom that changed your life. Those were the days! You had a wall of stress circuits, and some will remain, but all in all, you tore down that wall.

Now, more of the time, your prefrontal cortex has the capacity to attune to your emotional state, and think magnificent thoughts that light up the pleasure pathways in the brain. When those wild and wooly feelings crop up, you are fearless. You don't shut off the spigot of your emotions, but instead let them flow in highly effective ways. You have used the tools often enough and for long enough that you trust them. You know that if you process your emotions effectively, they will transform into exactly the balanced emotions—positive or negative—you need at that moment to nourish your spirit. That old numbness has become desire, and you rekindle that passion for life each time you use the tools. And you need that passion for it fuels your clarity and commitment to do what you came to earth to do.

That's what began happening for George and his family.

A MOMENT OF OPPORTUNITY

One day, George didn't appear for his appointment. I called his cell phone and was surprised to get no answer. I wondered if the baby had been born, and I knew my job was to wait. They would call when they were ready.

Then, two days later, Kate called asking for a coaching session, clearly upset.

"I need to do a cycle."

"By all means."

"Ace is having her baby right now, but she told me to stay out of it. The maternity ward is off limits. Ronald is in there with her, and I, her mother, am shut out."

"Are you ready for the flow of feelings?"

"I hate her for hating me. I am furious that the spoiled little witch is choosing her boyfriend over me. I hate it that she is shutting me out. I hate it that she is embarrassing me. All my friends go in with their daughters. But I am left out. I hate it that she is selfish. I can't stand it that the only person she cares about is herself. I hate that she is so damned spoiled. I can't stand that she always has to get it HER frigging way.

"Laurel, can you believe that she is shutting out her own mother?"

"You're doing a great cycle. Let it do its work for you."

"I hate it that she is so self-centered and childish. I hate that that I boiled chicken for her all these months, and washed her sheets, and folded her clothes—well, actually I supervised the housecleaner doing that—and I am so furious that right now that the most important event in my entire life is happening, and I'm missing it!

"I feel so sad that my daughter is having her baby and I'm out here in this hallway, locked out. I feel so sad and I feel afraid this is the start of her shutting me out of her life, out of my grandson's life, after all I've done. I hate it that I spoiled her. I hate it that she is so entitled! I feel sad for her. I feel sad for me. I feel afraid it will just get worse and I feel guilty . . ."

I waited.

"I don't feel guilty."

I waited longer.

"Well, my part of it is . . . I don't know. I feel guilty that I am selfish."

Now she could nab that errant stress circuit! I said, "And that would be completely reasonable because your basic expectation, the one wired long ago, during trauma or before the age of three was . . ."

"That it is all about me."

I sighed, knowing how hard she was working just to tolerate that thought.

"My basic expectation is that it is all about me."

MOVING TOWARD SPIRIT

"The reasonable expectation is . . ."

"It is NOT all about me."

I knew Kate could go deeper and create a new circuit that would be transformative, so I nudged her. "That would work if you were earlier in the training, Kate. At this point, you are more skilled. You are fully capable now of finding the eudonic reward, the reward of meaning here that will take you up and over and make this stressful experience a blessing."

She thought for a moment. I could hear her breathing in the telephone and people chatting in the background, sounds from the hall in the hospital from which she was calling.

I asked her, "What do you hold yourself accountable for? What is a reasonable expectation that will guide you to your joy, to your rewards of meaning that can quash any stress circuit and bury any loss in the dust?"

"I expect myself to hold on to my connection to myself, get to 1, and be a beacon of light in my daughter's life."

Kate had switched from ego to spirit. The joy from that one thought could swamp any of the stress Ace sent her way, as she evolved into a separate, loving, powerful woman.

I asked, "Positive, powerful thought?"

"That is the right thing."

I checked, "The essential pain?" In order for the new spiritual expectation to stick, she must identify and accept on an emotional level the loss, the lesson learned, the hard part.

"I am not in complete control. And when it is all said and done, Ace may reject me."

I exhaled. She had shifted her energy toward a state of balance and joy.

"The earned reward?"

"Well," she said. "The earned reward is that I have myself. Even if she rejects me, I won't reject me!"

"Yet for you, Kate, there is a reward that is your own, that makes your focused attention and follow-through meaningful; in fact, so meaningful that it quashes the circuits of stress. Poof, they disappear!"

"The rewards for me that warm my heart are integrity and spirituality."

Through the phone I could hear her exhale.

"Laurel," Kate said, "You know . . . I'm at 1."

A wave of love coursed through my body. "So am I."

We were quiet. The voices of people in the distant background in that hospital hallway sounded in my ear.

I asked Kate, "Where is George?"

She said with a small shiver of warmth in her voice, "He's here right next to me."

"Good. Can I talk with him?"

"Sure."

"George, how are you doing?"

His voice bellowed through the phone, "I'm in love."

"You're in love?"

"Yes. I'm in love with my life. I'm in love with my wife. And I'm in love with Ace, Ronald, and the baby—their baby, our grandson."

There would be more cycles to do, more circuits to rewire, but something had shifted in this big bear of a man.

"Will you send me a photo?"

"I'll e-mail you the photo as soon as possible. You'll be the first to see him."

George had become a beacon of light.

I hung up the phone, and thought, *How incredible it is that five simple tools could transform his life—and all their lives.*

Then, I cried. I cried and cried—for myself, for George, and for his family. I felt so grateful to be on this planet at this time, right now.

I thought of that little baby and hoped, just hoped that Ace's joy circuits and those of Ronald, Kate, and George, through their repeated contact over time, would be downloaded into his little brain, so that he could become his own beacon of light.

And who knows what could happen going forward? Perhaps he could move beyond stress symptoms, and feel so secure from within that he would have a wealth of compassion to send outward. Perhaps his small beacon of light could radiate outward and one beacon of light could alight another and another.

Until the last decade, none of us knew that there were universal tracks in the brain that could return us to well-being and that rolling, compassionate state of joy. We did not know the power of our focused, trained consciousness to transform the emotional terrain of our brains, to sculpt new pathways, and sequester old ones. Nor did we know that our intimate inner state could travel so freely from one brain to another so that our joy would be contagious and find its way into the emotional circuits of those around us. Now we do.

To the extent that we become wired for joy, we share our emotional wealth with others. Our joy makes us a beacon of light, spreading our positive emotional state to others in a natural contagion of warmth and compassion. One beacon of light shines on another and another, maybe, just maybe, beginning to create a world at 1.

Appendix A

Pocket Check In Card

Pocket Check In Card

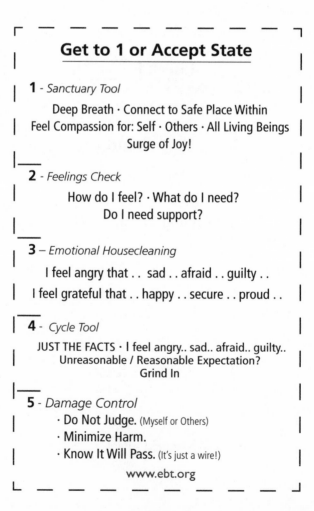

Get to 1 or Accept State

1 - *Sanctuary Tool*

Deep Breath · Connect to Safe Place Within
Feel Compassion for: Self · Others · All Living Beings
Surge of Joy!

2 - *Feelings Check*

How do I feel? · What do I need?
Do I need support?

3 – *Emotional Housecleaning*

I feel angry that . . sad . . afraid . . guilty . .
I feel grateful that . . happy . . secure . . proud . .

4 - *Cycle Tool*

JUST THE FACTS · I feel angry.. sad.. afraid.. guilty..
Unreasonable / Reasonable Expectation?
Grind In

5 - *Damage Control*

· **Do Not Judge.** (Myself or Others)
· **Minimize Harm.**
· **Know It Will Pass.** (It's just a wire!)

www.ebt.org

Additional EBT Resources

The purpose of this book is to introduce general readers to emotional brain training, which was developed at the University of California, San Francisco, beginning in 1979. If you are a provider or member of the science community who would like further information, you can access a detailed explanation of the science behind the method at www.ebt.org.

The emotional brain requires focused, intensive practice over time to gradually switch its emotional set point from stress to joy. These experiences are provided through six progressive EBT courses. Each course ("EBT Kit") builds on the rewiring accomplished in the previous course. In addition, each course focuses on the tools to create one of the six rewards. The courses are:

- **EBT Kit 1: Sanctuary:** Begin by sharpening your skills in the 5-Point System and experiencing more of the rewards of peace and power from within.

- **EBT Kit 2: Authenticity:** Build on that rewiring to experience more self-acceptance and greater authenticity. Rewire your first survival circuit to make it easier to change stress-fueled habits.

- **EBT Kit 3: Vibrancy:** Experience more joy in your daily life as you create a healthy lifestyle that is rich in natural pleasures. Erase another survival circuit that attaches you to stressed-out moods.

- **EBT Kit 4: Integrity:** With stress eased and the tools becoming more spontaneous, turn your attention to clarifying your purpose in life. Write a review of your life to heal old hurts and rewire a survival circuit that triggers merging or distancing.

- **EBT Kit 5: Intimacy:** With the wiring of a secure connection to yourself strong, experience more moments of intimacy in daily life: emotional connection, sensual pleasure, and loving companionship.

- **EBT Kit 6: Spirituality:** As stress symptoms fade and you have an abundance of all six rewards, notice that you are aware of the grace and mystery of life in a new way. You have become wired for joy.

The EBT community offers a range of support options for completing the six EBT Kits, including groups, telegroups, coaching, and retreats. In addition, support through technology is available, including e-courses, web-based tools, a social networking Website, and the EBT iPhone application. For more information, please visit www.ebt.org. For information on programs for preventing or treating childhood obesity through The Shapedown Program, please visit www.childobesity.org, www.shapedown.com, and www.youthevaluationscale.com.

All EBT providers are health professionals or educators who have completed personal and professional certification training in the method. For information about certification or to find certified providers in your community, please visit www.ebt.org. If you are a researcher who is interested in learning more about research collaborations, please e-mail research@ebt.org.

The Development of EBT

Beginning 30 years ago, a group of researchers at the University of California, San Francisco began to develop a method based on the premise that stress could be minimized through better control of the emotional brain. The first method was part of an interdisciplinary adolescent health-training program of national leaders in adolescent health directed by Charles E. Irwin, Jr. Later, in the Department of Family and Community Medicine—then directed by Jonathan Rodnick, with the research collaboration of Mary Croughan, and instrumental support from Marion Nestle—we adapted the method to emotional brain training for adults.

This method was originally inspired by a study published in 1940 by Hilde Bruch, a psychiatrist at Baylor College of Medicine, and her colleague, Grace Terrain, who observed patterns of permissiveness and deprivation in families with obese children. Our desire was to change not just the lifestyle behavior of obese children, but to find and address the root cause of their cravings. We drew on the work of Bruch and Terrain to develop skills based on good parenting—that is, warm nurturing, and consistent limits—and watched as children in the clinic, who were receiving this care, stop wanting the extra food. That program, Shapedown, has recently been updated to be consistent with the system described in this book and is used by medical practitioners and hospitals nationwide, and by the Canadian health system.

In the years that followed, we tested and applied this method through training and research with adults, working first with obesity and then with a range of addictive behaviors. Now the method is applied to rewiring the brain for a state in which the whole range of stress symptoms, addictions, and attachments fade, and the developmental rewards of life become abundant.

The research that has evaluated the effectiveness of EBT has shown remarkable effectiveness, including sustained post-treatment changes in a broad spectrum of stress-related variables. Most treatments typically show improvements during the process, with rapid return to pre-treatment levels afterward. Instead, with EBT, we have observed continued improvements in depression, blood pressure, weight, exercise, and other variables even as long as six years after training was completed.

More than 12 years ago, we established a nonprofit organization, the Institute for Health Solutions, to train and certify clinicians in this method and to facilitate its dissemination. Over the years, we have trained more than 500,000 people in the method, through certified providers who facilitate groups and coach, as well as through books and courses. My role has been to integrate research from a broad range of fields.

In the last three years, scientific breakthroughs have led to a new iteration of the method. It started as the Shapedown Program for children and adolescents, later evolved into an adult program known as The Solution Method, and now, with the advent of a new system that has broader applicability, emotional brain training. Not only is this new system simpler, it is more effective.

The prefiguring of *Wired for Joy* began in 2000, when EBT grew from tools based on family systems theory to integrating new understanding of positive emotional plasticity, which is how the emotional brain can change its functioning. A few years later, Igor Mitrovic, a neuroscientist and professor at the University of California, San Francisco, who teaches the sciences to medical and health professional graduate students, began using the method personally and became interested in the method's neuroscience. Before long,

Igor and I were speaking often. He began shepherding EBT to the next level of theoretical construct, and led the original training of medical students in the method. The "triangles" of neural circuitry that you will see in this book were of his design. Igor is now the Scientific Director of the Institute for Health Solutions. He is a source of inspiration and insight not only to me, but also to others who are leaders in this work, including Lindsey Fish, who specializes in neuroplasticity and EBT, Judy Zehr, who directs the method's clinical education, and the certified practitioners of the method, many of whom have contributed important ideas, suggestions, and research as the method has evolved.

EMOTIONS AND BRAIN PLASTICITY

Recent stress research has pointed to the nature of the stress response: how what you feel right now is not just the here-and-now stress, but also an accumulation of the effects of stress over time. Just knowing that enables you to shape an effective response, an unraveling of the past in pursuit of a new, joyful future. Using the tools of this method to clear away much of the emotional clutter—the wiring from past experiences—became core to the work.

This awareness was based on the research of three individuals: Bruce McEwen, a pioneer in stress research at Rockefeller University; internationally recognized stress researcher, Mary Dallman; and major contributor to the understanding of psychobiological stress mechanisms, Elissa Epel.

Although this method has been based on brain states since 2004, the work of Baylor College of Medicine's Bruce Perry, regarding the brain states of children of trauma, linked these states to specific brain regions. The work of Robert Sapolski, a professor of biology and neurology at Stanford University, has documented how chronic stress causes significant deleterious effects on every organ system in the body and exacerbates a range of physical and mental afflictions, including depression, anxiety, ulcers, colitis, heart disease, diabetes, obesity, immune diseases, memory loss, some cancers, and addictions. New York University's George LeDoux's research on the brain's fear centers and University of Southern California's Antonio Damasio's study of the nature of emotions informed our work in important ways. The Scripps Institute's George Koob's conceptualization of stress and addiction both enriched our work.

Recent research in neuroplasticity gave us insights about how to rewire brain circuits more easily and quickly. Work pioneered by Michael Merzenich of the University of California, San Francisco helped us begin to see that brain retraining may be as useful as drugs for some conditions. Daniel Siegel of the University of California, Los Angeles pioneered the application of concepts from attachment theory to mindfulness, work that contributed significantly to our thinking about this method. Mindfulness is a practice that has a range of forms, but Richard Davidson at the University of Wisconsin at Madison studied the brains of monks who have engaged in loving-kindness meditation. Jon Kabat-Zinn of the University of Massachusetts furthered the research in the area of mindfulness meditation and stress management. Harvard's George Valliant did elegant work on human development and, in particular, spiritual evolution, and University of California, Berkeley's Dacher Keltner made important inroads regarding the biologic basis for the role of positive emotions in spirituality and our very nature to strive to be good.

LOOKING FORWARD

Recently, a national coordinating center for research on this method was established at the University of California, San Francisco. The center works with other centers nationwide to facilitate further research on this method, which is known as emotional brain training in the scientific community. The Emotional Brain Training Center of Excellence is located in the Center for Health and Community at UCSF, which is directed by Nancy Adler, Professor of Medical Psychology. Since this method was originally developed to treat obesity in children and adults, the EBT center is also affiliated with the Center for Obesity Assessment, Study and Treatment (COAST), which focuses much of its work on the role of stress in the development, exacerbation, prevention, and treatment of obesity. Future directions include developing interventions for school-based preventive programs and for specific populations that are at risk. Additional research and training activities are key for this method to support its developing in being integrated into health care in the future.

Bibliography

The EBT method integrates three broad areas of science and builds on the work of many researchers. What follows are selected books that offer important insights and integrations of science that may be helpful in your understanding of the method.

Begley, Sharon. *Train Your Mind, Change Your Brain.* New York: Ballantine Books, 2007.

Cozolino, Louis. *The Neuroscience of Psychotherapy: Building and Rebuilding the Human Brain.* New York: W.W. Norton & Company, 2002.

Damasio, Antonio. *Looking for Spinoza: Joy, Sorrow and the Feeling Brain.* New York: Harcourt, 2003.

Doidge, Norman. *The Brain that Changes Itself: Stories of Personal Triumph from the Frontiers of Brain Science,* New York: Viking, 2007.

Flores, Philip J. *Addiction as an Attachment Disorder.* New York: Jason Aronson, 2004.

Goleman, Daniel. *Social Intelligence: Beyond IQ, Beyond Emotional Intelligence.* New York: Bantam Dell, 2006.

Haidt, Jonathan. *The Happiness Hypothesis: Finding Modern Truth in Ancient Wisdom.* New York: Basic Books, 2006.

Keltner, Dacher. *Born to be Good: The Science of a Meaningful Life.* New York: W.W. Norton & Company, 2009.

LeDoux, Joseph. *The Emotional Brain: The Mysterious Underpinnings of Emotional Life.* New York: Simon & Schuster, 1996.

Lewis, Thomas, Fari Amini, and Richard Lannon. *A General Theory of Love.* New York: Random House, 2000.

McEwen, Bruce. *The End of Stress As We Know It.* Washington, D.C.: Joseph Henry Press, 2002.

Sapolsky, Robert M. *Why Zebras Don't Get Ulcers: The Acclaimed Guide to Stress, Stress-Related Diseases, and Coping.* New York: Henry Holt, 2004.

Siegel, Daniel J. *The Developing Mind: How Relationships and the Brain Interact to Shape Who We Are.* New York: The Guilford Press, 1999.

———. *The Mindful Brain: Reflection and Attunement in the Cultivation of Well-being.* New York: W.W. Norton & Company, 2007.

Vaillant, George E. *Spiritual Evolution: A Scientific Defense of Faith.* New York: Broadway Books, 2008.

Acknowledgments

This book was a creative project that is grounded in the research, insights, and devotion of many people, to whom I am most indebted. Igor Mitrovic, the scientific director of the Institute for Health Solutions, has generously applied his understandings of neuroscience and physiology to moving the conceptual framework of the method. He has inspired us to explore the mysteries of the emotional brain in new ways, and move the method along to the next level of scientific rigor. I am deeply indebted to Igor, and relish our friendship and our collaborations.

Judy Zehr has been a constant source of insight about the role of attachment theory and EBT and has overseen clinical education on the method. Her brilliance shines through in the words of this book. Lindsey Fish dePeña's clarity and enthusiasm helped me through difficult times in the wiring of this book. Mary Croughan's guidance and support have been so important to the development of the method early on, even analyzing data on the method on the weekend.

The method would not have begun without Charlie Irwin's support in his adolescent health training program, and its transition into adult work was guided by the late Jonathan Rodnick, and with key support from Marion Nestle. To them, I am most grateful. I feel so fortunate for the sharing of Mary Dallman who has had a nurturing influence on the creation of this book, including sharing with me insights into the science of stress and the neurophysiology of the human brain. Nancy Adler has been instrumental in supporting us in developing an EBT national coordinating center in the Center of Health and Community (CHC). I am so grateful for her mentoring and support. Elissa Epel has given generously of her time and wisdom to support the development of this work, and her research on stress and obesity, in association with Center for Obesity Assessment, Study, and Treatment (COAST) has been invaluable. I am indebted to Kevin Grumbach, chair of the Department of Family and Community Medicine, and Sam Hawgood, chair of the Department of Pediatrics, for their support of this work. Mike Merzenich has been generous in his support of positive emotional plasticity, and his pioneering work in neuroplasticity has informed this work. I am grateful to Candace Pert, who has shown in her breakthrough research on opioid receptors that we were born for bliss. I am very grateful for the collaborations of Mary Charlson, M.D., and Janey Peterson, Ed.D., of the Center for Complementary and Integrative Medicine, Weill Cornell Medical College.

Deanne Hamilton, who has delivered the method for more than 20 years, continues to support health professionals in their certification in the method, and I am deeply grateful to her. Kelly McGrath has contributed important insights and has overseen the Institute for Health Solutions for more than eight years. Zack Small has orchestrated changes in our Internet presence and provided needed support. I appreciated their generosity and kindness. In addition, I am most grateful to those who have trained others in the method: Jackie Placidi, MSW, LMSW, Eastpoint, MI; Peggy Ernster, MN, RN, LPC, NCC, Glendale, AZ; Jill Shaffer, R.D., Pennington, NJ; Mary Killian, R.D., LD/N, Gainesville, Fla.; Carra Richling, R.D., Boulder, CO; Barbara McCarty, R.D., CD-N, Northford, CT; David Ingebritsen, Ph.D., LCPC, Benewah Medical Center, Plummer, ID; Bonnie Hoag, MFT, San Anselmo, CA; Susan Stordahl, LCSW, Corte Madera, CA; Alia Witt, R.D., MFT, San Diego, CA; Eve Lowry, R.D., Kaiser Hospital, Shingle Springs, CA; Sylvia Cramer, Ph.D., Redlands, CA; Connie Henderson, LCSW, Lee Vining, CA; Cynthia Moore, MS, R.D., CDE, FADA, University of Virginia, Palmyra, VA; Ellen Cohen, New York, NY, has coordinated the EBT Public Health Committee.

My colleagues at the University of California, San Francisco have offered important advice and support during recent years that have shaped the work, most particularly: Patty Robertson, Michele Mietus-Snyder, Liz Macera, Kari Connolly, Lynda Frassetto, Sue Carlisle, Andrea Garber, Amy Levine, Chelsea Simms, Vanessa George, Tracy Fulton, Joan Valente, Barbara Laraia, Kim McDermott, Joseph Castro, Andrew Parker, Lori Karan, Anna-Barbara Moscicki, Lee Ann Baxter-Lowe, Alka Kanaya, Brian Niehaus, Cam-Tu Tran, JoAnne Saxe, Robert Lustig, Anna

Spielvogel, Kristine Madsen, William Shore, Janet Wojcicki, Karen Parko, Felix Conte, Judy Moskowitz, and Mel Heyman. I am most grateful to Stuart Eisendrath for his support and insights on the method related to his own research on mindfulness-based stress reduction. I am thankful to Judi Mozesson, Anastasio Somarriba, Roy Johnston, Edgar Micua, Melanie Fisch, Kathy McHenry, Eli Puterman, Robert Wilson, Jana Toutolmin, Michael Thomas, Erica Gorman, Deanna Rutter, Nina Fry, and Bea Williams.

Bruce McEwen has been a wonderful source of wisdom in not only research but also care. I have been especially grateful to Dennis Styne for his support over the years including planning conferences at the University of California, Davis. Baylor College of Medicine's John Foreyt has encouraged and advised me throughout the years, University of California, Berkeley's Kristin Luker has offered valuable insights, and I am most grateful to Carl Greenberg, Rheinila Fernandes, Jane Rachel Kaplan, and John Gray for their contributions to the method. The support of Heather Frederickson and Barbara D'Elia for my research and professional development have been most appreciated. The Whitman Institute provided important support to the Institute in recent years and I am most grateful to John Esterle for his inspiration and guidance.

Laura Koch, my editor at Hay House, made countless improvements on the manuscript and nudged me to make the book tighter and more accessible. Her warm persistence and keen sense of what the reader needed vastly improved this work. I am deeply grateful to her. Patty Gift, director of acquisitions of Hay House, shared her enthusiasm for the work from the start. Sally Mason's warmth and attention to detail have been blessings. I am most grateful to them for guiding the book through its development. My agent, Bob Tabian, has offered a level of personal care and shepherding of this work, without which I believe it would never have been written. I am so grateful to him. Dede Taylor brought her insights and sensitivity to the book all along the way and contributed substantially to its editing. Sharon Wolbert edited the entire manuscript, drawing upon her knowledge of the method as an EBT coach and psychologist and giving of her time and her passion in remarkable and important ways. I am most indebted to her. The work began because of Bob Mellin's belief in publishing these ideas, and he continues to publish books on the method, The Shapedown Program, for obese children and adolescents. I am most grateful to him for now 30 years of support of this work. Jim Billings helped me understand the interweaving and spirituality and health, and his ideas and inspiration are imbedded in method.

Method providers who have supported this work in important ways include: Robin Anderson, R.D., Edmonton, Canada; Candy Cumming, MS, R.D., Sharp Hospital, El Cajon, CA; Sonia Elkes, R.D., San Carlos, CA; Misa Lawson, MPH, R.D., Santa Cruz, CA; Lynnie Sterba, LCSW, Redondo Beach, CA; Elizabeth Larkin, LCSW, Atlanta, GA; Neala Ausmus, LCPC, R.D., Springfield IL; Anne Nuss, M.Ed., LMHC, Wellesley Hills, MA; Andrea Wenger, R.D., CDE, Baltimore, MD; JoAnn Campbell, MS, LMHC, Yakima Valley Memorial Hospital, Yakima, WA; Denice Keepin, MA, LMHC, Seattle, WA; Kathleen Putnam, MS, R.D., Seattle, WA; Theresa Barry-Greb, PT, MS, Lexington, KY; Anne Strand, D.Min., LMFT, Oxford, MS; Sandra Martin, RN, MHS, Fenton, MO; Donna Hemingway, MS, Iowa City, IA; Terri Kirwan, MA, LPC, Louisville, CO; Kristie Salzer, MS, R.D., LD/N, Tampa, FL; Amy Licata, MS, LPCC, Greene Memorial Hospital, Miamisburg, OH; Susan Stanhope, LICSW, Wakefield, RI; Denise Kelley, MA, LPC, Asheville, NC; Cathirose Petrone, ND, CNC, Encinitas, CA; Karen Crane, CRNP, Mansfield, OH; Janet Chaize, MHC, Rush, NY; Liz Marushin, MFT Intern, Palos Verdes, CA; Laurence Freedom, M.Ed, LAC, LP, Lakewood, CO; Suzan Freedom, CAC-III, Arvada, CO; Michele Gorman, MS, R.D., LD, Wayzata, MN; Michelle Beller-Siegfried, MSW, Bellingham, WA; Aimee Gallo, HHC, San Diego, CA; Sherry Gaines, Ph.D., RN, College Park, GA; Gini Gardner, MFT, Kentfield, CA; Dede Taylor, MA, Weston, CT; Marian Stansbury, Ph.D., Milford, CT; Melanie Coles, R.D., Edmonton, Canada; Leslie Pruyn, LCPC, Aurora, IL; Gretchen Brickson, LCSW, Pasadena, CA; Elisabeth McKenna, Ph.D., Kaiser Hospital, San Jose, CA; Sharon Wolbert, Ph.D., Ridgewood, NJ; Margaret Norman, Richmond, VA; Nancy Rieben, R.D., L.D., Gainesville, GA; Diane Graves, R.D., Austin, TX; Mary D. Barry, CEAP, SPHR, Montpelier, VA;

Lois Vazirani, LCSW, BCDA, Rolling Hills Estates, CA; Richard Walker, BA, MA, Med, Richmond, VA; Jackie Sapp, LCSW, CEAP, Richmond, VA; Kristi Colbert, RN, BSN, PHN, Bayside, CA; Martha Simmons, M.D., Ph.D., Belmont, CA; Jean Pedersen, M.Ed., Ojai, CA; Teri Webb, Los Angeles, CA; Donna Foster, R.D., LD, Lexington, KY; Dorianna Shrader, Ph.D., Aurora, CO; Annika Kahm, BS, Stamford, CT; Frances O'Neil, R.D., MSW, Santa Ana, CA; Ilona Lichty, R.D., LD, Mount Vernon, IA; Dr. Amy Puls, Phoenix, AZ; Jennifer York, LMFT, Leucadia, CA; Melissa Swartz, BA, Martinsburg, WV; Jacalyn Thomas, M.Div., LCAS, Accokeek, MD; Nancy Franke Wilson, M.S., Plymouth, MN; Debra Lang, Psy.D., R.D., Bozeman, MT; Liz Shella, MA, LPC, CRC, Medina, OH; Judy Fitzgibbons, MS, R.D., LD, Cedar Rapids, IA; River Malcolm, LMFT, Eastsound, WA; Barbara Graf, MS, R.D., CD, Milwaukee, WI; Candi Dunbar, Redlands, CA.

Method mentors who have been generous with their time and support include: Betty Kasow, Anne Towery, David Rubnir, C. Aleck, Chris Hegge, George Whitehill, Janet Swisher, Jody King Colegrove, Karen Debusk, Kathy DeGrandis, Kim Moore, Kathleen Ryan, Linda Tyner, Linda Walling, Lisa Volk, Margaret Suddeth, Leitha Menegat, Nina Korican, Mary Lane, Sheila Comerford, Sue Druker, Sue Klapper, Sylvie Hebert, Judith Novakowski, Edie Winters, Annie Pohlenz, Patricia Lewis, Ann Sink, Susan Simmons, Kieran Bahn, Laura Uddenberg, Jeanne Gnuse, Harriet Hood, Amy Roe, Dan Helveston, Laura Revenko, Alison Vickery, Noelle Million, Anna Schroeder, Mary Urrutia, James Moline, Laura Doyle, Jennifer Deland, Tracy Hougum, and Sky Chari.

Many people have shared their expertise with our nonprofit institute and given of themselves in ways that have made this book possible, most particularly: Deborah Krupp, Rachel Fairbanks, Barbara Krohn, Cheryl Ridenour, Brandon McGrath, Jami Spittler, Gustave Loial, Warren Weagant, Kitt Weagant, Jill Johnson, Nina Hill, Dave Radlauer, Mary Crittenden, Bobbi Mullins, Tommy Odetto, Brett Mathiesen, Dawn Galbo, David Bott, Jim Cronin, Liz Levi, Teka Lutrell, William Taggart, Betsy and Bryant Young, Larry Townsend, Keith Parker, Dave Parker, Jill Schock, Susan Grabowski, Anne Huxley, Edna Gun Utter, Harry Elefther, Ed Garaventa, Sabrina Geshay, Nancy Bates,

Carol Duncan, Sean Maher, Meaghan Maher, Suzi and Rod Shoja, Suzi Lee Musgrove, and Nora Farnsworth. I am most grateful for the contributions of Dina Dudum, Marin Thompson, and Jennifer Taggart to this work, and to Colleen Mauro; Dee Niehaus; Mike Bell; Barbara and Gabrielle Muselli; Sharon Condy; David, Patti, and Cheryl Driggs; Kela and Carlos Cabrales; Hawley Riffenburg; Margery Greenberg; Janis Eggleston; Rob, Amy, Daniel, Matt, and Nicolas Forrest; Lisa Wilkins; Brian, Hailey, and Heidi Aicardi; Andrea Liguori; Louise Malandre; Ronda Goldman; Ann Vinson; Sharon Nielsen; and Terri Treat. I am most grateful to Ann Squires who has been extremely generous in contributing her consultation and support to the Institute to strengthen its infrastructure. Aeron Hicks consistently supported the method's development during challenging times, offering her support and devotion to the work and she, along with her husband Harold Hicks, shared important insights on the spiritual aspects of the method.

My mother passed away just as the ideas of the 5-point system became clear to us, yet she was aware that the book was in development and insisted that I keep the acknowledgments in the back of the book, and strive to be entertaining, rather than scientific. It is my hope that she would be pleased with this book and her contributions to it, as her love and passion are at the heart of this work. My dad had been a source of love and inspiration in my life, and after the passing of my mother he has shown our family how to be brave and strong in the face of losing one's ultimate love after 64 years of marriage.

The writing of this book was definitely a family affair. I am most grateful to each of my three children. I kept my son John Rosenthal's list of notes on what to remember when writing the book at my side throughout the process, and his loving and encouraging phone calls from college made me stronger. My son Joe Mellin has been a steady presence—planning, designing, and showing me how to change my thinking about the method and being instrumental in making the method more accessible through technology, design, and new perspectives. My daughter, Haley Mellin, has contributed artistically to the method over the years, and with this book gave of her heart and mind in ways that I will never forget. I am most grateful to my brother, Steve McClure, and his wife, Vivian, and their children, Sarah, Lisa, and Michael, for their support and our loving bond and good times. Veronica Lopez offered her warmth and her ideas about the importance of peace and compassion in the work. Harriet Pile, in her kind way, was integral to discussions about how the method should change. I have appreciated Zach Gold's calming ways and artistic insights. Priscilla Christopher has been a caring friend and important support. I am grateful for the friendship and many kindnesses of Lou Thoelecke; The Sharps: Andrea, JD, Sophie, and Sarah; Kathleen Wilson; Emily Kearney; Jock Begg; Kathleen and Kainoa Flickinger; Jena and Brett Walter; Aeron and Harold Hicks; Bonnie Hoag; Jane Cooper; Justine and Bruce Fairey; Marguerite Moriarty; Janice and Ralph Echenique; Heather Wallace; Mary Creigh Houts; Michael Rosendahl, and Meggie and Emily Rosendahl; Charlie Irwin, Nancie Kester, and Seth Kester-Irwin; Bernadette and Bruce Payne; Suzanne Danielson; Patricia Randolph; Dan Rosenthal; Tom Morrison; Travis Hayes; Emile Mulholland; Salvadore Romi; Irma Hernandez; Shilo Kantz; Mack Briggs; and Mike Mooney.

Anne Brown, a trainer and leader in the method, and a psychologist from Atlanta who passed away recently gave to the method with a full heart, developing training for the application of the method to those most in need, and always offering her sweet nurturing voice during our retreats and annual meetings. She continued to facilitate her telephone groups on the method up until a few weeks before her passing, because she said that doing this work nourished her spirit. During challenging times in the writing of this book I felt strengthened by my memories of her. I am grateful for the presence in my life of her husband, Beau, and their son, Julian.

Last, I am indebted to all the participants in the method who over the years have offered their advice, insights, and experiences in using the method that inspired us to continue exploring the grace and mystery of rewiring the emotional brain.

About the Author

Laurel Mellin is an associate clinical professor of family and community medicine and pediatrics at the University of California, San Francisco. She directs the national research coordinating center for emotional brain training (EBT) in UCSF's Center for Health and Community, which is affiliated with the Center for Obesity Assessment, Study and Treatment (COAST). She developed the Shapedown Program for pediatric obesity, which is used throughout the United States and by the Canadian Health Service, and the Youth Evaluation Scale (YES), an Internet-based assessment program for weight problems in the young.

Mellin has authored two bestsellers on the method; has trained psychologists, physicians, and other health professions on the method; and has conducted method research. She directs the nonprofit organization, The Institute for Health Solutions, which certifies health professionals in EBT. She has three children and lives in Marin County, California.

Website: www.ebt.org

Hay House Titles of Related Interest

YOU CAN HEAL YOUR LIFE, the movie,
starring Louise L. Hay & Friends
(available as a 1-DVD program and an expanded 2-DVD set)
Watch the trailer at: **www.LouiseHayMovie.com**

THE SHIFT, the movie, starring Dr. Wayne W. Dyer
(available as a 1-DVD program and an expanded 2-DVD set)
Watch the trailer at: **www.DyerMovie.com**

OOO

*ALL YOU EVER WANTED TO KNOW FROM HIS HOLINESS THE
DALAI LAMA ON HAPPINESS, LIFE, LIVING, AND MUCH MORE,*
by His Holiness the Dalai Lama

BE HAPPY: Release the Power of Happiness in YOU,
by Robert Holden, Ph.D.

*THE BIOLOGY OF BELIEF: Unleashing the Power
of Consciousness, Matter, & Miracles,*
by Bruce H. Lipton, Ph.D.

ELIMINATING STRESS, FINDING INNER PEACE,
by Brian L. Weiss, M.D.

EVERYTHING YOU NEED TO FEEL GO(O)D,
by Candace B. Pert, Ph.D.

All of the above are available at your local bookstore,
or may be ordered by contacting Hay House (see last page).

OOO

We hope you enjoyed this Hay House book. If you'd like to receive our online catalog featuring additional information on Hay House books and products, or if you'd like to find out more about the Hay Foundation, please contact:

Hay House, Inc., P.O. Box 5100, Carlsbad, CA 92018-5100

(760) 431-7695 or **(800) 654-5126**
(760) 431-6948 (fax) or **(800) 650-5115 (fax)**
www.hayhouse.com® • **www.hayfoundation.org**

○○○

Published and distributed in Australia by: Hay House Australia Pty. Ltd.,
18/36 Ralph St., Alexandria NSW 2015 • *Phone:* 612-9669-4299
Fax: 612-9669-4144 • www.hayhouse.com.au

Published and distributed in the United Kingdom by:
Hay House UK, Ltd., 292B Kensal Rd., London W10 5BE
Phone: 44-20-8962-1230 • *Fax:* 44-20-8962-1239
www.hayhouse.co.uk

Published and distributed in the Republic of South Africa by:
Hay House SA (Pty), Ltd., P.O. Box 990, Witkoppen 2068
Phone/Fax: 27-11-467-8904 • info@hayhouse.co.za
www.hayhouse.co.za

Published in India by: Hay House Publishers India,
Muskaan Complex, Plot No. 3, B-2, Vasant Kunj, New Delhi 110 070
Phone: 91-11-4176-1620 • *Fax:* 91-11-4176-1630
www.hayhouse.co.in

Distributed in Canada by: Raincoast, 9050 Shaughnessy St.,
Vancouver, B.C. V6P 6E5 • *Phone:* (604) 323-7100
Fax: (604) 323-2600 • www.raincoast.com

○○○

Take Your Soul on a Vacation

Visit **www.HealYourLife.com®** to regroup, recharge, and
reconnect with your own magnificence.
Featuring blogs, mind-body-spirit news, and life-changing
wisdom from Louise Hay and friends.

Visit **www.HealYourLife.com** today!